BOOK OUTLINE: THE HIDDEN ART OF PROMPT MASTERY

CHAPTER 1: THE CORE OF CURIOSITY

Word Count: 1500+

Summary:

In this chapter, we'll explore how curiosity shapes the nature of good prompts. Here, the emphasis is on how a curious mindset leads to better inquiries and what differentiates a surface-level prompt from one that digs deeper. We'll look at how to ask the right questions, embracing ambiguity, and constructing prompts that yield unexpected insights.

CHAPTER 2: FRAMING THE QUESTION – PRECISION VS. AMBIGUITY

Word Count: 1500+

Summary:

This chapter contrasts two fundamental approaches: sharp precision and controlled vagueness. We'll dive into when to use each method for the best results. It emphasizes understanding the context, purpose, and how to toggle between both for versatile outcomes in any scenario.

CHAPTER 3: LAYERED THINKING – BUILDING COMPLEXITY INTO SIMPLE PROMPTS

Word Count: 1500+

Summary:

Simplicity doesn't always mean shallow. In this chapter, we uncover how to layer multiple ideas, goals, and perspectives into even the simplest prompts. We'll explore how complexity can be infused without overloading, ensuring clarity while generating depth in responses.

CHAPTER 4: STRUCTURING THE FLOW – ORDER MATTERS

Word Count: 1500+

Summary:

The order of words and ideas significantly impacts the outcome of a prompt. This chapter explores the rhythm and sequence of information in prompts, explaining how structuring requests differently can yield varied, powerful results. We'll examine how the arrangement affects understanding and response generation.

CHAPTER 5: LANGUAGE PRECISION – THE SUBTLETY OF WORD CHOICE

Word Count: 1500+

Summary:

Words carry immense power. In this chapter, we delve into how the choice of specific terms, synonyms, and phrasings influences responses. We'll discuss how minor adjustments in language can pivot entire conversations and how synonyms with distinct connotations unlock different layers of understanding.

CHAPTER 6: FRICTIONLESS PROMPTS – REDUCING AMBIGUITY WITHOUT LIMITING SCOPE

Word Count: 1500+

Summary:

How do you create a prompt that is clear but not restrictive? This chapter uncovers the art of reducing unnecessary vagueness while keeping the door open for creative responses. It balances providing enough guidance without boxing in the answer.

CHAPTER 7: NUANCES OF CONTEXT – TAILORING PROMPTS TO SITUATIONS

Word Count: 1500+

Summary:

Context is king. This chapter emphasizes the importance of adapting prompts to specific situations, environments, and intentions. We'll look at how to integrate contextual hints into prompts, making them sharper and more tuned to specific needs, without over-explaining.

CHAPTER 8: THE POWER OF TONE – GUIDING WITH EMOTION AND STYLE

Word Count: 1500+

Summary:
Tone shapes perception. This chapter dives into how subtle shifts in tone can drastically affect responses. We explore using formality, warmth, excitement, or authority in prompts to steer the nature of the feedback, without relying on complex instructions.

CHAPTER 9: VISUAL IMAGERY – USING DESCRIPTIVE LANGUAGE FOR CLARITY

Word Count: 1500+

Summary:
When you need vivid responses, visual language makes a difference. In this chapter, we explore how using imagery within prompts can spark creative and detailed answers, enhancing both creative and analytical tasks. Descriptive language turns abstract concepts into concrete ideas.

CHAPTER 10: ITERATIVE REFINEMENT – EVOLVING YOUR PROMPTS

Word Count: 1500+

Summary:

Great prompts aren't born—they evolve. This chapter looks at how the art of refinement leads to better outcomes. We explore how to assess prompt effectiveness, adjust wording, and sharpen focus through iteration. It's a lesson in patience and fine-tuning for richer responses.

CHAPTER 11: LEVERAGING EXAMPLES – GUIDING WITHOUT DICTATING

Word Count: 1500+

Summary:

Sometimes showing is better than telling. This chapter explains how using examples in prompts can guide understanding without stifling creativity. We explore how to strike the perfect balance between showing the direction and giving enough freedom for open interpretation.

CHAPTER 12: INDIRECT GUIDANCE – SUBTLE STEERING THROUGH SUGGESTION

Word Count: 1500+

Summary:

Indirect methods of control often yield the most creative results. This chapter explores the art of subtlety in prompt design, where you guide responses without overt direction. By hinting, nudging, or offering gentle constraints, we'll explore how prompts can lead responses down creative, unexpected paths.

CHAPTER 13: INTERDISCIPLINARY PROMPTS – BORROWING FROM THE ARTS, SCIENCES, AND MORE

Word Count: 1500+

Summary:
Prompts that pull from different fields lead to more robust and varied responses. This chapter explores how to blend concepts from the arts, sciences, literature, and philosophy to create more nuanced and multi-faceted prompts that push boundaries.

CHAPTER 14: ANTICIPATING RESPONSES – THE ART OF REVERSE ENGINEERING

Word Count: 1500+

Summary:

Mastering prompts means predicting potential outcomes. This chapter reveals how anticipating answers helps refine the way questions are posed. It's a look at reverse engineering prompts to maximize effectiveness, guiding you to think ahead about the types of answers desired.

CHAPTER 15: THE ART OF SILENCE – KNOWING WHEN TO SAY LESS

Word Count: 1500+

Summary:

Less can indeed be more. This final chapter focuses on the art of brevity and minimalism in prompts, showing that sometimes, the most powerful prompts are the ones that say just enough to spark deep thinking, without overwhelming the responder.

Closing Thoughts: *Embracing the Art*

Summary:

A brief conclusion that wraps up the book by encouraging readers to view prompting not just as a skill, but as an ongoing art form—one that evolves with practice, curiosity, and insight. The key takeaway is that prompt mastery isn't about perfection but about continual exploration.

CHAPTER 1: THE CORE OF CURIOSITY

Curiosity is often misunderstood as simply a desire to know more, but when it comes to crafting effective prompts, it is the **driving force** behind both questions and the insights that follow. In prompt design, curiosity isn't just a mental state—it's a **strategic tool**. This chapter will explore how you can tap into the art of curiosity, fine-tune it, and use it to sculpt better prompts that lead to deeper, more insightful responses.

The Nature of Curiosity

To master prompts, one must first grasp the nature of curiosity itself. **Curiosity** is not a one-size-fits-all mentality; it can be broad, open-ended, or hyper-focused depending on the desired outcome. When crafting prompts, curiosity begins with intention—knowing what you want to uncover.

Is the goal to generate an **outpouring of ideas**, explore **unknown territory**, or seek a **specific solution**? Each of these goals requires a different kind of curiosity:

- **Exploratory curiosity** seeks novelty. Prompts that tap into this often ask open-ended questions or explore hypothetical scenarios.
- **Solution-driven curiosity** is more targeted, looking for efficiency or a clear, actionable answer. These prompts are sharper and more focused.
- **Reflective curiosity** probes deeper into thoughts and feelings, seeking to understand motivations and underlying patterns.

Understanding which type of curiosity to channel is the first step toward crafting a truly effective prompt.

Constructing Curiosity-Driven Prompts

Now that we understand the varieties of curiosity, the question becomes: How do we craft prompts that reflect it?

1. Start with a Core Question

Every prompt should begin with a central question, one that embodies the core of the curiosity driving it. But here's the secret: **Don't settle for the first question that comes to mind.** Push beyond it. The surface question might be simple: "How can we improve X?" But a deeper question would be: "What underlying assumptions about X have we missed in our efforts to improve it?"

By **challenging assumptions**, the prompt immediately moves from basic inquiry to one that digs into the unknown.

2. Layer in Specificity

Once you've developed the core question, add layers of specificity. The best prompts focus curiosity by narrowing down broad questions to manageable pieces without closing off avenues of exploration. This is the sweet spot where curiosity thrives—enough clarity to spark meaningful responses, but enough room for creative freedom.

For example, instead of asking:

● *"How do we make work more efficient?"*

Consider:

● *"What small, overlooked habits in daily work routines are holding back efficiency, and how might we subtly shift them?"*

This version sharpens the question's focus, narrowing down on **specific behaviors**, while still encouraging creative input. It leverages curiosity by assuming there are hidden inefficiencies waiting to be uncovered.

3. Encourage Open Exploration

An important part of nurturing curiosity is crafting prompts that allow for **open exploration** without overwhelming the responder. **Questions that begin with 'What if,' 'How might,' or 'In what**

ways' are powerful triggers for exploration. They signal to the respondent that creativity and outside-the-box thinking are not only welcomed but necessary.

For instance:

- *"What if our approach to problem X was entirely wrong? How might we start over without preconceived notions?"*

This opens up new avenues of thought by removing constraints, urging the respondent to abandon safe, linear thinking in favor of **exploring new possibilities**.

The Role of Curiosity in Eliciting Unexpected Insights

The most effective prompts lead to answers that surprise both the asker and the responder. How? By tapping into a **curiosity-driven feedback loop**. The best prompts don't just ask for knowledge— they generate new questions in the mind of the responder. In turn, this inspires them to dig deeper, not only answering the prompt but also unearthing new layers of understanding.

One trick to harnessing this feedback loop is by building prompts that **challenge the responder's assumptions**. A question like:

- *"What's one thing you know about this problem that you're sure is true—but might actually be wrong?"*

forces the responder to interrogate their own knowledge base. This type of prompt goes beyond standard curiosity; it generates a **curiosity spiral** where one question leads to further inquiry, making it far more likely to yield fresh insights.

Balancing Curiosity with Direction

While curiosity drives a prompt's exploratory potential, **too much vagueness** can lead to a lack of focus, resulting in unhelpful responses. The key is to **balance curiosity with direction**.

Take this example:

- *"What are potential future trends in technology?"*

While it's open-ended, it may not lead to useful, focused responses. On the other hand:

- *"How might consumer behavior shape the direction of wearable technology in the next five years?"*

This version gives respondents a **clear target** while still leaving room for their curiosity to stretch and explore. The prompt remains focused, but encourages creative and informed responses.

Curiosity vs. Confidence in Prompt Responses

An intriguing dynamic arises when you begin to realize how curiosity and confidence can interplay within prompts. Some prompts that nurture curiosity can lead to hesitant or **tentative responses**—the respondent might not be sure of their answer, but the question itself leads them to further exploration. Alternatively, prompts that aim to affirm existing knowledge can be framed to evoke confident, **declarative responses**.

Consider:

- *"What's one possible outcome if this method fails?"*

This question nudges the respondent to consider **uncertainty** and invites speculative responses. Conversely:

- *"Based on past experience, what's the most reliable method to achieve X?"*

This prompt aims to evoke a more **assertive** response, drawing on the respondent's confidence and expertise.

The Key to Mastery: Curiosity in Practice

Ultimately, mastering prompt engineering is about understanding how to wield curiosity in a way that elicits deeper responses. As with any skill, it's honed through practice and refinement. By asking better, more curious questions, you'll receive more thoughtful and meaningful responses.

In Conclusion

Curiosity is the **backbone of effective prompts**. Whether you're probing for hidden insights, sparking creative ideas, or seeking clarity in ambiguity, the secret lies in how you channel curiosity. With practice, you'll not only learn to craft better questions but also to unlock richer answers that go beyond surface-level thinking. **Prompt mastery** is a dance between guiding curiosity and allowing it room to breathe.

CHAPTER 2: FRAMING THE QUESTION – PRECISION VS. AMBIGUITY

A well-constructed prompt must walk a fine line between precision and ambiguity. Too much precision, and the response may be limited, overly narrow, or formulaic. Too much ambiguity, and the response may be vague or unfocused. The key is understanding when each approach is most effective and how to blend both in a way that generates nuanced, insightful results.

In this chapter, we'll dive deep into the art of framing a question, focusing on **how to wield precision and ambiguity** strategically in the world of prompt design.

The Power of Precision

Precision in prompting is about **clarity** and **focus**. It's the difference between asking:

- *"What do you think about technology?"*
- versus:
- *"How has wearable technology transformed the way we interact with our surroundings?"*

The second version narrows the scope, ensuring that responses will be **specific** and actionable. Precision helps eliminate the possibility of vague, wandering answers by guiding the respondent toward a particular point of discussion. This approach is particularly useful when you need **concrete** answers, data-backed insights, or actionable steps.

When to Use Precision

Precision is most effective in the following contexts:

1. **Tackling Complex Problems**:
   When you're dealing with highly complex subjects, precision helps break down the problem into manageable parts. For instance, instead of asking:

   o   *"What's the solution to global warming?"*

2. You might ask:

   o   *"What specific steps can local governments take to reduce emissions in urban areas within the next five years?"*

3. This prompts the respondent to zoom in on a focused part of the issue, producing a response that is grounded and more likely to lead to actionable insights.
4. **Requesting Actionable Information**:
   If you're seeking direct advice or suggestions, precision is key. Vague questions will often produce vague answers. Compare:

   o   *"How do I improve my writing?"*
   o   with:
   o   *"What techniques can I use to make my sentences more concise while maintaining clarity?"*

5. The latter question invites responses that offer tangible methods, tools, or techniques.
6. **Avoiding Misunderstanding**:
   Sometimes, ambiguous prompts leave too much room for interpretation, resulting in responses that don't meet your needs. For example:

   o   *"What's the future of work?"*

7. This could lead to answers about anything from automation to remote working trends. But if you ask:

o   *"How will AI integration change office-based jobs in the next decade?"*

8. You're directing the response toward a specific aspect of the future of work, minimizing potential miscommunication.

How to Craft Precise Prompts

1. **Be Clear and Concise**:
    Don't overwhelm the prompt with too many details. Precision comes from clarity, not complexity. Aim to ask **one focused question** per prompt.
    Example:

o   *"What's one overlooked benefit of this method?"*

2. **Use Direct Language**:
    Avoid vague terms like "stuff," "things," or "some." Instead, use direct language that leaves no room for interpretation.
    Example:

o   *"What are the top three strategies you recommend for managing time during product development?"*

3. **Ask for Specific Outcomes**:
    When you want particular kinds of answers—like numbers, percentages, or timelines—state this clearly in your prompt.
    Example:

o   *"Provide a five-step plan to launch a startup in the fintech sector."*

The Role of Ambiguity

Ambiguity, when used correctly, is a **powerful tool** in prompting. It allows the respondent room to **interpret**, to **think creatively**, and to explore a **range of possibilities**. While precision narrows the focus, ambiguity opens the door to broader, more diverse answers.

Consider the prompt:

- *"What could the future of transportation look like?"*

This is intentionally ambiguous, allowing for speculation about **technology, policy, urban design**, and even **environmental concerns**. Such prompts are designed to inspire **imagination** and **exploration**. Ambiguity encourages the respondent to look beyond the obvious, to consider different angles, and to bring in unique perspectives.

When to Use Ambiguity

Ambiguity is best suited for:

1. **Exploring New Ideas**:
   When the goal is to generate **creativity** or **brainstorm** new concepts, ambiguity is your ally. Prompts like:

○ *"In what ways might AI and human creativity collaborate?"*

2. allow the respondent to consider various possibilities without being boxed in by overly specific guidelines.
3. **Provoking Deep Thought**:
   Ambiguous prompts often lead to deeper, more reflective answers. When you want to push the respondent to **think critically**, ambiguity provides the space for deeper consideration.
   Example:

○ *"What's the role of failure in achieving success?"*

4. This prompt encourages philosophical reflection, rather than a simple right-or-wrong answer.
5. **Allowing Interpretation**:
   Some topics benefit from the respondent bringing their own **interpretation** to the table. Ambiguity invites different perspectives and interpretations, making it an excellent tool for discussions that thrive on **diversity of thought**.
   Example:

○ *"What does innovation mean in a post-pandemic world?"*

25

6. Each respondent might interpret "innovation" differently, leading to a variety of insights.

How to Craft Ambiguous Prompts

1. **Keep It Open-Ended**:
   Ambiguity thrives in open-ended questions. Avoid framing the prompt in a way that implies only one correct answer.
   Example:

   o *"How could human society evolve in the next century?"*

2. **Use Broad Terms**:
   Incorporate broad terms like "future," "possibilities," or "potential" to allow more room for interpretation.
   Example:

   o *"What possibilities could arise from a world without borders?"*

3. **Encourage Speculation**:
   Prompts that encourage speculation allow the respondent to imagine scenarios and make predictions.
   Example:

   o *"If money were no object, how might education systems change?"*

Blending Precision and Ambiguity

The real artistry of prompting comes when you learn to blend **precision and ambiguity** to achieve optimal results. Some prompts benefit from a mixture of both: being precise enough to give direction, but ambiguous enough to inspire creativity.

For instance:

• *"How can wearable technology improve human life in the next decade, particularly in healthcare and personal fitness?"*

This prompt is **precise** in the sense that it narrows down the focus to **wearable technology**, **healthcare**, and **personal fitness**, but it also leaves room for **imagination** by asking how these areas might be improved, a question that encourages forward-thinking and creative solutions.

Examples of Balanced Prompts

Balanced Prompt 1:

- *"What technological advancements are likely to shape the future of education, and how might they impact learning for both students and teachers?"*

This prompt is **specific** about education and the impact on **both students and teachers**, but **ambiguous** enough to allow for speculation on what technologies will emerge.

Balanced Prompt 2:

- *"What unexpected consequences could arise from widespread automation in the workforce, both positive and negative?"*

The prompt is **precise** about focusing on **automation** in the workforce, but leaves room for a **wide range** of consequences, ensuring varied and thoughtful responses.

CONCLUSION: FINDING THE RIGHT BALANCE

In mastering prompts, knowing when to be precise and when to embrace ambiguity is key to eliciting the most valuable responses. **Precision** creates clarity, ensuring that responses are relevant and actionable, while **ambiguity** invites creativity and exploration, leading to unexpected and diverse insights. The art of prompting lies in knowing which approach to use—and when a blend of both might yield the most powerful results.

The next step in our journey will dive deeper into how to layer complexity into seemingly simple prompts, ensuring that you can create questions that, while short in form, are rich in substance.

CHAPTER 3: LAYERED THINKING – BUILDING COMPLEXITY INTO SIMPLE PROMPTS

One of the hidden secrets to mastering prompts lies in the ability to craft **simple questions** that yield **complex answers**. This technique, which we'll call **layered thinking**, involves embedding multiple layers of thought, intent, and direction into a single, well-crafted prompt.

In this chapter, we'll uncover how to incorporate layers of complexity into seemingly simple prompts and how this subtle art can lead to **richer, more nuanced responses**.

The Concept of Layering in Prompts

At its core, **layered thinking** in prompt design is about embedding multiple goals or angles within a single prompt. It's like giving a question depth without making it appear complicated on the surface. The result? You'll get answers that touch on a variety of aspects, offering you insights that go far beyond what a straightforward question would elicit.

Consider the difference between these two prompts:

1. *"What is the role of leadership in a team?"*
   vs.
2. *"In what ways does leadership impact team dynamics, decision-making, and conflict resolution?"*

While both questions are simple, the second prompt introduces **layers** by mentioning specific aspects of team function—**dynamics**, **decision-making**, and **conflict resolution**. The added layers encourage the respondent to consider the topic from multiple perspectives, prompting a **richer** and **more detailed** answer.

Why Layering Matters

Layering prompts helps generate answers that are:

- **Multidimensional**: By embedding several angles in a question, you receive responses that cover a range of considerations, ensuring you don't miss out on valuable insights.
- **Thought-provoking**: Layered prompts encourage respondents to **think critically**, as they must address more than one aspect of the problem.
- **Engaging**: Respondents tend to find layered prompts more engaging because they are **challenging** and require deeper thinking.

How to Create Layered Prompts

Layered prompts don't have to be complex to be effective. In fact, simplicity is often the best disguise for complexity. Here's a step-by-step guide to crafting layered prompts:

---

1. Start with a Core Theme

Every layered prompt begins with a **core theme** or **central idea**. This is the foundation upon which you'll build your layers. The core theme could be broad, such as "leadership," "technology," or "innovation."

For example, let's take the theme of **sustainability**.

---

2. Add Strategic Layers

Once you have your core theme, you can start adding layers by introducing **specific elements** that help deepen the inquiry. These layers could be:

- **Subtopics** (e.g., sustainability in terms of economic impact, social responsibility, environmental effect)
- **Processes or stages** (e.g., how sustainability influences planning, execution, and review)
- **Perspectives or stakeholders** (e.g., government, corporations, consumers)

Consider this layered prompt on sustainability:

- *"How can sustainability be integrated into corporate strategy, and what impact does it have on both long-term financial goals and stakeholder relationships?"*

Here, the core theme is **sustainability**, but there are two clear layers—**corporate strategy** and the **impact on financial goals and stakeholders**. The prompt encourages a response that explores the topic from different angles, ensuring a more nuanced discussion.

---

3. Use Connective Phrases

To tie your layers together, use **connective phrases** that ensure the question feels cohesive and smooth. Common phrases that work well in layered prompts include:

- *"In what ways does... affect..."*
- *"How might... influence..."*
- *"What impact does... have on..."*

For example:

- *"How might emerging technologies influence education, particularly in the areas of accessibility, personalized learning, and teacher-student interaction?"*

This question brings in **emerging technologies** as the core theme, but then explores specific areas like **accessibility**, **personalized learning**, and **teacher-student interaction**, providing multiple layers for the respondent to consider.

---

4. Balance Focus and Flexibility

While layering adds depth, you must also be careful to balance **focus** and **flexibility**. A prompt that's too rigid might lead to predictable answers, while one that's too loose might result in scattered or unfocused responses.

A well-layered prompt maintains clear **boundaries** (so the respondent knows exactly what you're asking), while still allowing room for interpretation. You want to guide the conversation without dictating every detail.

Consider this example:

- *"What are the challenges and opportunities of remote work in terms of productivity, work-life balance, and team collaboration?"*

It's clear that the prompt is asking about **remote work**, but the layers of **productivity**, **work-life balance**, and **team collaboration** allow for flexibility in how the respondent chooses to approach the question.

Examples of Layered Prompts

Let's break down a few examples to illustrate how layered prompts work:

Example 1: Innovation and Society

- *"How does innovation in healthcare impact patient care, healthcare costs, and the role of medical professionals?"*

Core Theme: Innovation in healthcare
Layers: Patient care, healthcare costs, role of medical professionals
Effect: This prompt encourages the respondent to consider the effects of innovation from different angles—both practical and professional—leading to a more complete analysis.

Example 2: Leadership and Culture

• *"In what ways can leadership styles shape workplace culture, employee engagement, and conflict resolution strategies?"*

Core Theme: Leadership styles
Layers: Workplace culture, employee engagement, conflict resolution
Effect: The prompt invites a response that discusses leadership's broad impact while focusing on specific areas that contribute to a well-rounded answer.

Example 3: Technology and Education

• *"How can digital tools enhance educational outcomes, and what are the challenges in implementing them across diverse learning environments?"*

Core Theme: Digital tools in education
Layers: Educational outcomes, challenges in diverse learning environments
Effect: This prompt balances exploration of benefits (enhancing outcomes) with a discussion of practical challenges, encouraging a balanced and thorough response.

The Art of Asking Follow-Up Questions

Layered prompts are also a great way to generate **follow-up questions**. A layered response often touches on multiple ideas, any one of which could be explored further.

For instance, take this prompt:

• *"How does urban design influence environmental sustainability, community well-being, and economic growth?"*

A thoughtful response to this question might touch briefly on each of the three layers. However, you could follow up with more detailed questions like:

- *"How does urban design specifically impact community well-being in lower-income neighborhoods?"*
- *"What are the economic trade-offs when prioritizing sustainability in urban planning?"*

Layering not only deepens the initial response, but it creates opportunities for even richer, more insightful discussions through strategic follow-ups.

The Benefits of Layered Prompts

Layered prompts offer several key advantages:

1. **Depth of Response**: You're more likely to get detailed, thoughtful answers that touch on multiple aspects of the subject, leading to deeper insights.
2. **Efficiency**: By layering questions, you can ask about several aspects of a topic in one go, making your prompts more efficient and time-effective.
3. **Encouraging Connections**: Layered prompts encourage respondents to make connections between different ideas, fostering more creative and critical thinking.
4. **Clarity and Focus**: Despite the complexity of the answers they produce, layered prompts can still maintain a sense of clarity and direction, ensuring responses stay relevant.

Conclusion: Simplicity with Depth

Layered thinking in prompt engineering is all about making sure that your questions, while seemingly simple, contain enough complexity to produce insightful answers. This allows respondents to explore multiple angles, dig into details, and make connections they might not otherwise consider.

In the next chapter, we'll explore how the **order** of information presented in a prompt can further influence the depth and clarity of responses, building on the layers we've just discussed.

CHAPTER 4: STRUCTURING THE FLOW – ORDER MATTERS

The order in which you present information within a prompt can profoundly impact the quality and direction of the responses you receive. Just like in storytelling, where the sequence of events can change the reader's experience, in prompt design, structuring the flow of a question can shape the respondent's understanding, clarity, and focus.

In this chapter, we'll explore the importance of flow, how to structure prompts to elicit the best responses, and how sequencing affects the depth and relevance of answers.

The Importance of Flow in Prompts

Think of a prompt like a **conversation**. The way you structure your question guides the thought process of the respondent. Good flow ensures that the respondent is introduced to concepts gradually, leading them toward deeper, more focused responses. Poor flow, on the other hand, can lead to confusion, missed points, or superficial answers.

Flow is about **guidance**. When crafting a prompt, you are guiding the respondent through an idea, laying down stepping stones that lead them from point A to point B. Each piece of the prompt builds on the last, encouraging the respondent to **think critically** and **logically**.

The Components of Effective Flow

To master prompt flow, it's crucial to understand its components. A well-structured prompt typically involves three elements:

1. **Context**: The background or framing of the question. Context provides the foundation that ensures the respondent understands what you're asking and why it matters.
2. **Focus**: The core of the prompt that directs the respondent to the specific aspect you want them to explore. This is where you clearly state what you're asking for.
3. **Depth**: The layers or nuances that deepen the question, prompting the respondent to think beyond surface-level answers and explore more meaningful insights.

Let's break down how to use these components to structure effective prompts.

---

1. Providing Context First: Setting the Stage

Context is the information or background that frames the question. Without context, prompts can seem **random** or **vague**, leading to irrelevant or shallow responses.

Consider the following two prompts:

1. *"How can companies improve employee morale?"*
    vs.
2. *"In a rapidly changing work environment, where remote work and flexible schedules are becoming the norm, how can companies improve employee morale?"*

In the second prompt, the added context sets the stage, providing crucial background that helps guide the respondent toward more **relevant** and **specific** answers. The context provides a shared understanding of the environment in which the question is being asked, reducing ambiguity and ensuring the respondent knows exactly where to focus.

How to Add Effective Context:

- **Frame the Problem**: Before diving into the main question, offer a brief setup that introduces the issue or topic.
Example:
  - *"With the increasing demand for renewable energy sources, how can governments balance economic growth with environmental sustainability?"*
- **Establish Relevance**: Help the respondent understand why the question matters, whether it's due to current trends, challenges, or broader implications.
Example:
  - *"As digital transformation accelerates in various industries, how can small businesses adapt to stay competitive in the global market?"*

Context doesn't have to be long or complicated. Even a sentence or two is often enough to establish the necessary foundation.

---

2. Sharpening the Focus: Directing the Response

Once you've set the context, it's important to guide the respondent toward the specific **aspect** of the topic you want them to explore. This is where you shift from the general to the specific.

Without clear focus, you risk receiving a wide range of responses, many of which may not be relevant. Focus narrows the scope, ensuring that the respondent addresses the key issue or question you care about.

For example:

- *"In what ways can technology be used in education?"*
vs.
- *"How can interactive digital tools, like virtual labs or simulations, enhance student engagement in STEM education?"*

The second prompt has a sharp focus. Instead of leaving the respondent to speculate broadly about technology in education, it directs them to think about specific tools and outcomes. The result? A more targeted, useful response.

How to Sharpen Focus:

- **Ask for Specific Aspects**: Guide the respondent by focusing on a particular area within the broader topic.
Example:
  ○ *"What role does user experience play in the success of mobile applications, particularly in terms of retention and user satisfaction?"*
- **Define the Scope**: Be clear about the boundaries of the question. Focus helps prevent responses that veer off-topic.
Example:
  ○ *"How can non-profit organizations leverage social media for fundraising without compromising their core mission?"*
- **Use Precise Language**: Make sure the language of your prompt is precise, avoiding vague terms like "things" or "stuff" and instead specifying what you're asking for.
Example:
  ○ *"What are the most effective marketing strategies for reaching Gen Z consumers through Instagram and TikTok?"*

---

3. Adding Depth: Encouraging Critical Thinking

After you've established context and focus, it's time to layer in **depth**. This is where you encourage the respondent to think critically, to consider nuances, and to offer more insightful responses.

Depth is what elevates a basic prompt into one that sparks thoughtful, **meaningful discussions**. It encourages the respondent to go beyond the obvious and explore underlying themes, consequences, or relationships.

For instance:

- *"What are the benefits of renewable energy?"*
vs.
- *"What are the long-term benefits of transitioning to renewable energy sources, particularly in terms of environmental sustainability and economic development?"*

The second prompt goes deeper by asking the respondent to consider both **environmental** and **economic** factors, which adds layers of complexity and encourages a more well-rounded response.

How to Add Depth:

- **Incorporate Multiple Dimensions**: Invite the respondent to consider the question from more than one angle or to explore both pros and cons.
Example:
  ○ *"How might automation impact job markets, considering both the potential for job loss and the creation of new opportunities?"*
- **Ask for Relationships**: Encourage the respondent to consider how different elements interact or influence each other.
Example:
  ○ *"What is the relationship between corporate culture and innovation, and how can leaders foster a work environment that promotes creative thinking?"*
- **Prompt for Long-Term Thinking**: Encourage the respondent to think beyond immediate results and consider long-term implications.
Example:
  ○ *"How could urban planning decisions made today affect the sustainability and livability of cities over the next 50 years?"*

The Role of Order in Prompt Structure

The order in which you present context, focus, and depth affects the **clarity** and **flow** of the prompt. Here's why the right sequence matters:

- **Building Understanding**: Context comes first because it helps the respondent understand the topic before they dive into specifics. Without context, the respondent might misunderstand the purpose of the prompt.
- **Focusing the Answer**: After the context is established, the focus ensures the respondent knows **what to address**. Without focus, responses can become broad and miss the point.

- **Encouraging Thoughtfulness**: Finally, depth prompts the respondent to think beyond the surface and offer a **well-rounded**, thoughtful response. Without depth, answers may be too simple or lacking in substance.

Example of Good Flow:

Let's look at an example of a prompt with excellent flow:

- *"As climate change continues to threaten coastal regions, many cities are investing in flood defenses. However, rising sea levels and increased storm intensity are making it harder to keep up. What strategies can local governments adopt to both protect their cities in the short term and create sustainable, long-term solutions for future generations?"*
- **Context**: The first sentence sets the stage by explaining the issue of climate change and the investments cities are making.
- **Focus**: The second sentence narrows the scope, highlighting the specific challenges of sea levels and storm intensity.
- **Depth**: The final question introduces depth by asking for both short-term and long-term solutions, ensuring the response is comprehensive.

Conclusion: Mastering the Flow

Mastering prompt flow is essential for getting high-quality responses. By carefully structuring prompts to include **context**, **focus**, and **depth**, you create questions that are clear, engaging, and thought-provoking. The order in which you present these elements shapes the respondent's understanding and encourages richer, more insightful answers.

In the next chapter, we'll dive into the nuances of **word choice** and how subtle shifts in language can influence the outcome of your prompts, transforming good questions into great ones.

CHAPTER 5: LANGUAGE PRECISION – THE SUBTLETY OF WORD CHOICE

Language is more than just a vehicle for communication—it's a tool that can influence perception, guide thought, and shape responses. In the realm of prompt design, every word counts. The precision of your language can mean the difference between a focused, meaningful answer and one that's broad, vague, or off-topic.

In this chapter, we'll explore how careful word choice plays a pivotal role in prompting, how subtle shifts in phrasing can transform responses, and how to leverage the power of language to elicit clearer, more valuable insights.

The Power of Word Choice

In prompt design, your **word choice** acts as a compass, directing the respondent's thinking and approach to the question. The right words provide clarity, invoke specific associations, and set the tone for the response.

Consider these two prompts:

1. *"How do people feel about remote work?"*
2. *"What are the psychological effects of remote work on employee well-being?"*

The first prompt is vague, leaving the door open to a wide range of responses. The second prompt uses precise language—**psychological effects** and **employee well-being**—which frames the question in a more focused and meaningful way. The second version is likely to produce deeper, more specific responses because it clarifies the angle of inquiry.

Precision vs. Vagueness

Language precision is all about reducing ambiguity while maintaining **relevance**. While ambiguous prompts can lead to creative answers (as we discussed earlier), in many cases, precision helps bring **clarity** and **focus** to responses.

Take the following example:

- *"How do businesses use technology?"*
vs.
- *"In what ways do businesses use artificial intelligence to improve customer service and operational efficiency?"*

The second prompt uses **precise terms**—artificial intelligence, customer service, operational efficiency—which guides the respondent to consider specific technologies and outcomes, leading to a more **relevant** and **focused** answer.

Understanding the Impact of Keywords

Certain **keywords** can frame a question in ways that affect the scope of the answer. In prompt engineering, it's essential to be intentional about the words you choose, particularly when you're aiming for specific types of responses.

Here are some examples of how keywords can influence the direction of a response:

1. **Quantitative vs. Qualitative**

   ○ Quantitative: *"What percentage of your budget is allocated to marketing?"*
   ○ Qualitative: *"How do you prioritize your budget when it comes to marketing?"*

2. In the first example, the use of "percentage" invites a numerical answer. In the second, the phrase "how do you prioritize" opens the door for a more qualitative, reflective response. The word choice here directs the respondent toward either hard data or subjective reasoning.

3. **Time-Bound Phrasing**

○   *Immediate*: *"What immediate steps can we take to address this issue?"*
○   *Long-Term*: *"What long-term strategies should we consider to solve this issue sustainably?"*

4. These two prompts both address the same issue but have vastly different timelines. Words like **immediate** and **long-term** shift the focus to actions that are either urgent or future-oriented, which will shape how the respondent thinks about their answer.

5. **Action-Oriented vs. Reflection-Oriented**

○   *Action*: *"What steps should we take to increase employee engagement?"*
○   *Reflection*: *"How has employee engagement evolved in the company over the last five years?"*

6. Action-oriented prompts call for **solutions** and **next steps**, while reflection-oriented prompts ask for **analysis** and **review**. Choosing between action and reflection depends on the type of response you're looking for—whether it's a plan for the future or an understanding of past trends.

Strategic Use of Synonyms

Even minor shifts in vocabulary can have a significant impact on how a prompt is understood. Different words may have similar meanings, but their connotations and **associations** can subtly alter the nature of the response. The following pairs of synonyms illustrate this point:

1. **Consequences vs. Impacts**

○ *"What are the consequences of implementing this policy?"*
○ *"What are the impacts of implementing this policy?"*

2. The word **consequences** carries a slightly negative tone, which may lead the respondent to focus on potential downsides. In contrast, **impacts** is more neutral, leaving room for both positive and negative interpretations.
3. **Challenges vs. Opportunities**

○ *"What are the challenges of remote work?"*
○ *"What opportunities does remote work present?"*

4. While **challenges** invites a discussion of obstacles or difficulties, **opportunities** shifts the focus to potential benefits or new possibilities. Choosing one over the other can shape the overall direction of the conversation.

Crafting Tone Through Language

Language doesn't just convey information—it also conveys **tone**. The tone of a prompt can influence how a respondent feels about the question and the depth of their response. A prompt with a **formal tone** might elicit more serious, analytical responses, while a **conversational tone** could lead to more open-ended or casual answers.

Compare these two versions of the same question:

● *"What are the critical components of a successful marketing campaign?"*
vs.
● *"In your opinion, what makes a marketing campaign successful?"*

The first version has a more **formal** tone, implying an academic or technical answer. The second version feels **conversational**, encouraging the respondent to share their personal perspective. Tone can affect not only the type of response you receive but also the **comfort level** of the respondent in answering.

How to Control Tone:

1. **Use of Pronouns**:
   The use of "you" or "your" tends to create a more informal, conversational tone, while avoiding personal pronouns keeps things more formal.
   Example:

   ○ *Formal*: *"What factors contribute to success in project management?"*
   ○ *Conversational*: *"What do you think makes a project successful?"*

2. **Question Framing**:
   The way you frame a question can set the tone for the response. More direct, formal questions often imply a certain level of seriousness or importance.
   Example:

   ○ *Formal*: *"Analyze the impact of automation on the workforce."*
   ○ *Conversational*: *"How do you think automation will affect jobs in the future?"*

Using Contrast to Focus Responses

In some cases, contrasting ideas or outcomes within a single prompt can sharpen the focus of the response. By presenting two or more options, you guide the respondent to compare, contrast, and evaluate the differences.

For instance:

● *"What are the advantages and disadvantages of adopting a hybrid work model in large corporations?"*

Here, the respondent is invited to consider both **pros and cons**, ensuring that the answer covers multiple dimensions of the question. Contrast-driven prompts encourage more **balanced** and **thoughtful** responses.

Examples of Contrast-Driven Prompts:

- *"How does remote work impact productivity and work-life balance?"*
- *"What are the benefits and challenges of using open-source software in enterprise settings?"*
- *"Compare the short-term and long-term effects of climate change policies on economic growth."*

In each case, the contrasting elements push the respondent to consider multiple perspectives, leading to a richer, more comprehensive response.

Balancing Simplicity with Depth

While language precision often involves being specific and clear, there's also a need to balance **simplicity** with **depth**. A question that's too complex might overwhelm the respondent, while a question that's too simple might not lead to the depth of insight you're looking for.

Consider:

- *Overly complex*: *"What are the sociocultural, economic, and technological influences that have driven the evolution of leadership practices in multinational corporations over the past three decades, and how do these factors interplay with global trends in corporate governance?"*
- *Overly simple*: *"How has leadership changed in recent years?"*

Both extremes have their pitfalls. A well-crafted prompt balances simplicity with depth by using precise language that is easy to understand, yet invites a thoughtful, detailed response.

How to Balance Simplicity and Depth:

- **Simplify Structure, Not Content**:
Keep the structure of your prompt simple, but make sure the content invites deeper thinking.
Example:
  - *"What role has technology played in shaping consumer behavior over the last decade, and what trends might emerge in the next five years?"*
- **Break Complex Ideas into Manageable Parts**:
Instead of asking a highly complex question in one go, break it into smaller parts that guide the respondent to address each element without feeling overwhelmed.

Conclusion: The Precision Paradox

Precision in language doesn't mean complexity—it means **clarity**. The best prompts are those that use simple, precise language to ask nuanced questions. By being intentional about word choice, you can guide respondents toward the insights you're looking for without over-explaining or leading them in predictable directions.

In the next chapter, we'll look at how to create **frictionless prompts**—those that are clear, open-ended, and inviting without becoming too vague or ambiguous.

CHAPTER 6: FRICTIONLESS PROMPTS – REDUCING AMBIGUITY WITHOUT LIMITING SCOPE

Creating prompts that are clear and focused, yet open enough to inspire creative and thoughtful responses, is a delicate balance. The goal is to reduce unnecessary **ambiguity** that can confuse or overwhelm the respondent, while still allowing enough **freedom** for them to explore ideas fully.

In this chapter, we'll explore the art of designing frictionless prompts—those that **guide without constraining**, offer **clarity without oversimplification**, and invite **thoughtfulness without leading** the respondent too rigidly.

The Problem with Over-Ambiguity

Ambiguity, while useful in sparking creativity, can also lead to **confusion** if not managed properly. When a prompt is too ambiguous, it may leave the respondent unsure of what's being asked, resulting in either unfocused or superficial answers.

Take the following example:

- *"How can businesses be more innovative?"*

While the question allows for broad interpretation, it might be **too** open, leaving the respondent wondering:

- What kind of businesses?

- What aspect of innovation—products, processes, or culture?
- What's the specific goal of innovation—profits, sustainability, or customer experience?

This kind of ambiguity often results in answers that are **too broad** to be useful, or they miss key aspects you were hoping to explore.

The Art of Reducing Ambiguity

To reduce ambiguity while maintaining scope, you need to ensure that your prompt is **clear**, **focused**, and **actionable**, but without closing off creative avenues. Here's how to strike that balance:

---

1. Be Clear About the Topic

The first step in reducing ambiguity is making sure the **core topic** of the prompt is clear. The respondent should immediately understand the **subject** you want them to address.

Consider these two examples:

1. *"How do organizations improve their processes?"*
   vs.
2. *"How do large tech companies improve their product development processes to stay competitive in the market?"*

In the second prompt, the focus is clearer: it specifies **large tech companies** and **product development processes**, while still leaving room for a variety of potential strategies. The prompt is frictionless because it's **clear**, yet not overly restrictive.

How to Add Clarity:

- **Define the Subject**: Instead of asking about a general topic, clearly define the **who** or **what** involved in the prompt.
Example:
  - *"What are the most effective marketing strategies?"*
  - **Refined**: *"What are the most effective digital marketing strategies for e-commerce companies targeting millennials?"*

In the refined version, the focus on **digital marketing, e-commerce companies**, and **target audience** (millennials) adds clarity, ensuring that the response is relevant without being overly specific.

---

2. Ask Focused, Actionable Questions

Frictionless prompts give the respondent a **clear action** to focus on, which helps reduce unnecessary ambiguity. While you want to leave room for interpretation, providing a **direction** is crucial to avoid vague answers.

Example:

- *"How do companies handle change?"*

vs.

- *"What strategies do companies use to successfully navigate large-scale organizational changes, and how do they measure the effectiveness of these strategies?"*

The refined version asks for specific **strategies** and invites the respondent to think about **measurement**—two clear, actionable aspects that focus the response while still allowing room for creativity.

How to Make Questions Actionable:

- **Use Directive Phrases**: Phrases like "What strategies," "In what ways," or "How do" prompt the respondent to provide **specific actions** or methods.

Example:

- *"In what ways can public policy drive renewable energy adoption in urban areas?"*
- **Refined**: *"What policies can local governments implement to increase renewable energy adoption in urban areas, and how can they ensure community engagement?"*

The refined version maintains scope by focusing on **policies** and **local governments** while still encouraging the respondent to think about community engagement.

3. Offer Parameters Without Being Restrictive

While you want to give direction, offering too many constraints can stifle creativity. Frictionless prompts provide **parameters**—guidelines that give the respondent a sense of focus—without becoming **overly restrictive**.

For instance:

- *"What are the best practices in business management?"*
vs.
- *"What are the best practices in managing remote teams, particularly in terms of communication, productivity, and employee well-being?"*

The second version gives **clear parameters** (remote teams, communication, productivity, employee well-being), but it's not so restrictive that it limits the respondent's ability to explore various strategies. It's broad enough to encourage creative responses, but narrow enough to avoid an overwhelming range of answers.

How to Offer Parameters:

- **Narrow the Focus with Categories**: Specify key categories or areas of focus, but avoid listing too many at once.
Example:
  ○ *"What are the challenges of launching a startup?"*
  ○ **Refined**: *"What are the financial and operational challenges of launching a startup in the technology sector?"*

This provides clear categories (financial and operational challenges) but still leaves room for interpretation and exploration.

---

4. Maintain Open-Ended Flexibility

Frictionless prompts often allow for **open-ended** responses, encouraging the respondent to explore different possibilities. However, too much openness can result in a lack of focus. To maintain flexibility without sacrificing clarity, use **open-ended** phrasing that still suggests a clear line of thinking.

For example:

- *"What might the future of transportation look like?"*
vs.
- *"In what ways might the development of autonomous vehicles impact urban infrastructure and public transportation in the next decade?"*

The second prompt is open-ended in that it allows the respondent to speculate on future developments, but it still provides **specific areas** to focus on (urban infrastructure, public transportation). This creates a balance between **flexibility** and **focus**.

How to Maintain Open-Ended Flexibility:

- **Use "What if" or "In what ways" Phrasing**: These phrases invite exploration but within a specific context or theme.
Example:
  ○ *"In what ways might advancements in artificial intelligence reshape healthcare delivery and patient care?"*

This prompt allows for speculation while still guiding the respondent to focus on **healthcare delivery** and **patient care**.

Avoiding Leading Questions

While reducing ambiguity is important, you also want to avoid creating **leading questions**—prompts that push the respondent toward a particular answer or conclusion. Leading questions can stifle original thinking and result in biased responses.

For example:

- *"Don't you think remote work is more productive than office work?"*

This question clearly leads the respondent toward a specific answer. A better version would be:

- *"How do you think remote work compares to office work in terms of productivity, collaboration, and work-life balance?"*

The revised version avoids bias by asking the respondent to consider multiple factors without suggesting a preferred outcome.

How to Avoid Leading Questions:

- **Avoid Yes/No Questions**: These questions tend to box the respondent into a specific answer. Instead, ask open-ended questions that encourage exploration.
Example:
  o *Leading*: *"Is sustainability important for business growth?"*
  o **Improved**: *"In what ways can sustainability drive business growth, and what are the potential challenges?"*
- **Present Multiple Perspectives**: When appropriate, ask the respondent to consider more than one angle or perspective.
Example:
  o *"What are the benefits and drawbacks of using automation in customer service?"*

Examples of Frictionless Prompts

Let's look at a few examples of prompts that strike the right balance between clarity and flexibility, reducing ambiguity while still allowing for creativity:

1. **General Topic**: *Sustainability in Business*

o *"How can companies in the retail sector adopt more sustainable practices without compromising profitability, and what challenges might they face in doing so?"*

2. **Why It Works**: This prompt provides clear parameters—**sustainable practices, retail sector, profitability**—but still invites the respondent to explore challenges and possible solutions creatively.
3. **General Topic**: *Education*

○   *"In what ways might virtual reality and augmented reality tools enhance student engagement in science education, and what are the potential limitations of these technologies?"*

4. **Why It Works**: This prompt is clear about the **technologies** and **subject area** (science education) while allowing for a discussion of both **benefits** and **limitations**.
5. **General Topic**: *Innovation and Technology*

○   *"How might advances in quantum computing change industries such as finance, healthcare, and logistics over the next 20 years?"*

6. **Why It Works**: The prompt focuses on **quantum computing** and specific **industries** (finance, healthcare, logistics) but gives the respondent flexibility to explore future impacts.

Conclusion: The Art of Frictionless Prompts

Frictionless prompts achieve the delicate balance of being clear enough to provide **direction**, while still being open-ended enough to allow for **creative exploration**. By offering parameters without over-constraining, and by focusing on clarity without leading the respondent toward a particular conclusion, you create prompts that foster thoughtful, nuanced, and insightful responses.

The key to crafting frictionless prompts is understanding how to **guide without limiting**—to reduce ambiguity but leave space for interpretation and creative thinking. By using **clear language**, providing **actionable focus**, offering **open-ended flexibility**, and avoiding **leading questions**, you can craft prompts that generate responses that are not only relevant but also rich in detail and diversity of thought.

In the next chapter, we'll explore the nuances of **contextual adaptation**—how to tailor prompts to different situations, audiences, and purposes to maximize their effectiveness.

CHAPTER 7: NUANCES OF CONTEXT – TAILORING PROMPTS TO SITUATIONS

A key aspect of mastering prompt engineering is understanding how to adapt prompts to suit different **contexts**. Just as an artist tailors their brush strokes depending on the canvas, prompt engineers must adjust the scope, tone, and structure of prompts based on the situation and audience. Whether you're crafting prompts for creative exploration, solving complex problems, or driving professional outcomes, knowing how to tailor your approach is critical.

In this chapter, we'll explore how context informs prompt design and how to shape prompts for various situations, whether they are academic, creative, professional, or analytical.

Why Context Matters

The effectiveness of a prompt is often determined by the **situation** in which it is used. Context includes:

- **Audience**: Who is answering the prompt? What is their background and knowledge level?
- **Purpose**: Why are you asking this question? Are you seeking specific information, creative ideas, or critical analysis?
- **Environment**: Where is this prompt being used? In a business meeting, a classroom, or a brainstorming session?

Tailoring your prompts to fit the **context** ensures that the responses you receive are relevant, thoughtful, and aligned with the goals of the situation.

Let's break down how context influences prompt design.

---

1. Tailoring Prompts for Professional Settings

In professional environments, prompts are often designed to **solve problems**, **make decisions**, or **drive performance**. Here, clarity, precision, and relevance are paramount. Professionals tend to value efficiency, so the prompts need to be direct, actionable, and tied to **business outcomes**.

Example of Professional Context:

- **General Prompt**: *"How can we improve customer satisfaction?"*
- **Contextualized Prompt for a Business Meeting**: *"What specific improvements can our customer service team implement to enhance customer satisfaction by 15% over the next quarter?"*

Why It Works: This prompt is tailored to a professional audience by providing **clear objectives** (enhancing customer satisfaction by 15%) and a **timeframe** (next quarter). It pushes the respondent to think in terms of concrete actions that can be implemented.

Key Strategies for Professional Contexts:

- **Set Clear Objectives**: Ensure the respondent knows exactly what outcome or result is being sought.
Example:
  o *"What strategies can we use to reduce operational costs by 10% while maintaining quality standards?"*
- **Include Timelines or Metrics**: Adding time constraints or measurable goals ensures that the responses focus on practical, actionable steps.
Example:
  o *"How can our team increase quarterly sales revenue by 20% without increasing our marketing budget?"*
- **Use Action-Oriented Language**: Words like **implement**, **strategize**, and **optimize** indicate that you are looking for solutions,

not just ideas.
Example:

o   *"What improvements can we implement to streamline our internal communication systems?"*

---

2. Adapting Prompts for Creative Exploration

In contrast to professional settings, creative environments thrive on **imagination, innovation**, and **open-ended thinking**. Here, prompts should encourage respondents to think outside the box, challenge norms, and explore **multiple possibilities**.

Example of Creative Context:

- **General Prompt**: *"What are some new product ideas?"*
- **Contextualized Prompt for a Creative Brainstorming Session**: *"Imagine we had an unlimited budget and no technical restrictions—what wild, futuristic product could we design that would revolutionize how people interact with technology?"*

Why It Works: This prompt encourages **imaginative thinking** by removing constraints (unlimited budget, no restrictions) and using vivid language like **wild** and **futuristic**. It opens the door for creative exploration, giving participants the freedom to dream big.

Key Strategies for Creative Contexts:

- **Use Imaginative Language**: Encourage creative responses by using words that spark the imagination, such as **dream, imagine**, and **what if**.
Example:

o   *"What if cities could float? How might that change the way we think about urban design and architecture?"*

- **Remove Practical Constraints**: Creative prompts often work better when typical limitations (budget, time, resources) are temporarily removed to let ideas flow freely.
Example:

o   *"If you could invent anything with no budget constraints, what would it be and why?"*

- **Encourage Speculation**: Asking participants to speculate on possibilities that don't yet exist opens up the potential for **radical innovation**.
Example:
  - *"How might the rise of virtual reality transform education in ways we can't yet fully imagine?"*

---

3. Shaping Prompts for Academic and Analytical Purposes

In academic or analytical contexts, the focus is often on **critical thinking**, **problem-solving**, and **evidence-based responses**. Prompts should encourage depth, rigor, and structured thought, guiding respondents to consider **multiple perspectives**, **analyze data**, or explore theoretical implications.

Example of Academic Context:

- **General Prompt**: *"Discuss the impact of climate change."*
- **Contextualized Prompt for an Academic Essay**: *"Analyze the long-term economic effects of climate change on coastal communities, considering both the risks and potential adaptation strategies that could mitigate these impacts."*

Why It Works: This prompt encourages the respondent to take a **deep dive** into a specific issue, asking for analysis of **long-term effects** and **adaptation strategies**. It's framed to provoke a more structured and **evidence-based** response.

Key Strategies for Academic and Analytical Contexts:

- **Ask for Multiple Perspectives**: Encourage respondents to consider **different viewpoints** or **competing theories** to develop a more nuanced analysis.
Example:
  - *"How do Marxist and capitalist economic theories differ in their approaches to global poverty reduction?"*
- **Focus on Analysis and Evidence**: Instead of simply asking for an opinion, ask respondents to **analyze** data, provide evidence, or

evaluate consequences.

Example:

o   *"Analyze how income inequality has evolved in the United States since the 1970s, using data from at least three major studies to support your argument."*

• **Include Comparisons or Contrasts**: Analytical prompts often benefit from **comparisons**, encouraging the respondent to evaluate two or more factors in relation to each other.

Example:

o   *"Compare the social and economic impacts of renewable energy adoption in developing nations versus developed nations."*

---

4. Tailoring Prompts for Problem-Solving Scenarios

Problem-solving prompts focus on addressing specific challenges or issues, requiring solutions that are **practical**, **innovative**, and **feasible**. Whether in a business, academic, or personal context, these prompts should encourage the respondent to identify problems and propose **actionable solutions**.

Example of Problem-Solving Context:

• **General Prompt**: *"How can we improve team collaboration?"*
• **Contextualized Prompt for a Business Problem-Solving Session**: *"What specific tools and processes can we implement to improve cross-departmental collaboration, particularly between marketing and product development teams, while minimizing communication bottlenecks?"*

Why It Works: The prompt clearly defines the **problem** (cross-departmental collaboration) and asks for **specific tools and processes** to solve it, focusing the respondent on actionable solutions.

Key Strategies for Problem-Solving Contexts:

• **Frame the Problem Clearly**: Make sure the respondent understands the exact problem they're addressing by providing sufficient **context**.

Example:

o   *"How can we reduce product delivery times by 20% without increasing costs or sacrificing quality?"*

- **Ask for Specific Solutions**: Ensure the respondent knows that you are looking for **concrete actions** or strategies, rather than just general ideas.

Example:

o   *"What three strategies can we implement to improve employee retention over the next 12 months?"*

- **Encourage Consideration of Obstacles**: Problem-solving often involves overcoming challenges. Ask respondents to think about both the solution and the **potential barriers** to implementation.

Example:

o   *"What steps can we take to scale our operations internationally, and what challenges should we anticipate in terms of legal compliance and logistics?"*

---

5. Customizing Prompts for Personal Reflection or Growth

When prompts are used for **personal growth** or **self-reflection**, they should be introspective, open-ended, and designed to prompt **honest exploration** of thoughts and feelings. These types of prompts should encourage the respondent to think deeply about their experiences, challenges, or values.

Example of Personal Reflection Context:

- **General Prompt**: *"What motivates you?"*
- **Contextualized Prompt for Personal Development**:
"Reflecting on your personal and professional life, what experiences have most shaped your sense of purpose, and how do these experiences continue to influence your decisions today?"

Why It Works: This prompt invites a **deep reflection** on personal experiences and **long-term influences**. It encourages the respondent to explore both the past and the present, making for a richer and more meaningful reflection.

Key Strategies for Personal Reflection:

- **Ask for Specific Experiences**: Personal reflection prompts work best when they invite the respondent to focus on **specific moments** or experiences that shaped their growth.

Example:

- *"Think of a time when you faced a significant challenge. How did you overcome it, and what did you learn about yourself in the process?"*
- **Encourage Self-Awareness**: Prompts that ask respondents to reflect on their motivations, values, or decisions can encourage greater self-awareness and insight.
Example:
  - *"What personal values guide your decision-making, and how have these values evolved over time?"*
- **Leave Room for Emotional Exploration**: Allow space for respondents to explore their emotions, thoughts, and feelings without feeling constrained by specific guidelines.
Example:
  - *"When you think about your professional journey, what moments have brought you the most joy, and why do they stand out to you?"*

---

6. Adapting Prompts for Group Settings

When crafting prompts for **group discussions** or **team brainstorming**, it's important to design them in a way that encourages **collaboration** and ensures that all voices can contribute. Group prompts should invite multiple perspectives and leave room for open-ended conversation.

Example of Group Discussion Context:

- **General Prompt**: *"How can we improve company culture?"*
- **Contextualized Prompt for a Group Workshop**: *"What three initiatives could we introduce to improve company culture, and how*

can each team member contribute to making these initiatives successful?"

Why It Works: This prompt not only invites ideas for improvement but also encourages participants to consider their own role in implementing solutions, fostering a sense of **ownership** and **collaboration**.

Key Strategies for Group Contexts:

- **Invite Multiple Perspectives**: Group prompts should encourage participants to consider different viewpoints or ideas, fostering a rich discussion.
Example:
  o *"What are some different ways we could approach problem-solving in our team, and how can each approach benefit our overall workflow?"*
- **Encourage Collaboration**: Prompts that invite collaboration can lead to more dynamic discussions. Ask participants to build on each other's ideas.
Example:
  o *"What initial steps can we take to launch this project, and how can different departments collaborate to ensure its success?"*
- **Keep It Open-Ended**: In group settings, open-ended prompts allow for a range of contributions, ensuring that the discussion remains inclusive.
Example:
  o *"What new processes could we introduce to streamline communication between our teams, and how can we ensure everyone is on board with these changes?"*

The Importance of Audience Awareness

Whether you're crafting prompts for **students, professionals, creative teams**, or **individuals reflecting on personal growth**, understanding the **audience** is key. Tailoring your prompts to the audience's level of knowledge, expertise, and emotional readiness ensures that the responses are relevant and insightful.

For instance:

- **Expert Audience**: For highly knowledgeable professionals, you can use **specific terminology** and ask for **detailed** or **technical** insights.
Example:
  - *"How can advanced machine learning algorithms be applied to optimize supply chain management?"*
- **General Audience**: For a broader audience with varying levels of expertise, simplify the language and focus on **accessible ideas**.
Example:
  - *"What role can technology play in improving the efficiency of supply chains?"*

Understanding your audience ensures that your prompts are engaging and aligned with their level of understanding and interest.

Conclusion: Tailoring Prompts for Maximum Impact

The **nuances of context** are essential to crafting effective prompts. Whether you're targeting professionals, creatives, students, or individuals on a personal journey, adapting your prompts to the specific context helps ensure that the responses are relevant, thoughtful, and meaningful.

By considering the **audience**, **purpose**, and **environment**, you can create prompts that guide respondents toward insightful answers while allowing for creativity and exploration. Tailoring prompts is an ongoing process—one that involves constantly adjusting and refining your approach to meet the needs of different situations.

In the next chapter, we'll explore the power of **tone** and how adjusting the tone of a prompt can influence the nature of the response.

CHAPTER 8: THE POWER OF TONE – GUIDING WITH EMOTION AND STYLE

The **tone** of a prompt can significantly impact the response it elicits. Tone shapes the mood, directs the level of formality, and influences the way respondents engage with the question. Whether you want a lighthearted and creative reply or a serious and analytical response, the way you set the tone can guide your audience toward the type of answers you're looking for.

In this chapter, we'll explore the different types of tone, how to adjust tone to fit the purpose and audience, and how to use tone to subtly influence the quality and depth of the responses you receive.

What is Tone in Prompt Design?

Tone refers to the **emotional quality** or **attitude** conveyed through your language. It reflects how you want the respondent to feel when they engage with your prompt and can range from formal to informal, serious to playful, or enthusiastic to neutral. Tone not only affects how respondents interpret the question, but also how they approach answering it.

Compare these two prompts:

1. *"What is the biggest challenge facing modern education?"*
2. *"In your opinion, what's the toughest hurdle education systems are facing today, and how do you think we can fix it?"*

Both prompts ask a similar question, but their tones differ:

- The first is more **formal** and academic, which may elicit a more structured and objective response.
- The second is **conversational** and personal, which may encourage a more relaxed and subjective answer.

Why Tone Matters

Tone matters because it shapes the **respondent's expectations**. A serious tone may encourage a well-thought-out, detailed response, while a playful tone might lead to more creative or casual answers. The tone you choose should match the **purpose** of the prompt and the **audience** you are addressing.

For instance:

- **Professional Settings**: A formal tone is often more appropriate, as it signals that the respondent should provide serious, thoughtful answers.
- **Creative Brainstorms**: A lighter, more playful tone can encourage creativity and risk-taking, making respondents feel more comfortable offering unconventional ideas.
- **Personal Reflection**: A compassionate or empathetic tone helps create a safe space for respondents to share more personal or introspective thoughts.

Types of Tone and Their Effects

Let's break down several common types of tone and explore how they affect responses.

---

1. Formal Tone

A **formal tone** is often used in professional or academic contexts where precision, clarity, and professionalism are essential. It tends to invite more **structured** and **rigorous** responses.

Example of Formal Tone:

- *"What are the key factors that influence employee retention in large organizations, and how can management address these factors effectively?"*

This prompt is **serious** and **to the point**, suggesting that the respondent should provide a well-reasoned, analytical response. Formal tone is best used when you're looking for **data-driven** answers or professional opinions.

When to Use a Formal Tone:

- **In business reports, proposals, or research inquiries**: This tone signals that the topic is important and requires a thoughtful, **objective** response.
- **In analytical or evaluative prompts**: Formal tone encourages respondents to **focus on facts** and **evidence**, avoiding emotional or subjective bias.

Impact:
Respondents are likely to provide **organized, fact-based** answers that are thorough and professional.

---

2. Conversational Tone

A **conversational tone** is more casual, often using **personal pronouns** like "you" and "your." This tone is useful when you want to create a sense of dialogue or engagement, making the prompt feel more **approachable** and **relaxed**.

Example of Conversational Tone:

- *"What do you think are the biggest challenges businesses are facing these days, and how would you handle them?"*

Here, the prompt feels like part of a **friendly conversation**, encouraging the respondent to share their personal perspective. Conversational tones are effective in **informal settings** where creativity and personal opinions are encouraged.

When to Use a Conversational Tone:

- **In brainstorming sessions**: This tone makes respondents feel **comfortable** expressing creative ideas without fear of judgment.
- **In personal or reflective prompts**: When asking respondents to share their opinions, experiences, or feelings, a conversational tone invites them to be more **candid** and **open**.

Impact:
Respondents are likely to offer **personal, subjective** insights that feel authentic and relaxed.

---

3. Playful or Humorous Tone

A **playful tone** injects **fun** into the prompt, making it lighthearted and entertaining. This tone is especially useful when you want to **break down barriers** and encourage **creative thinking** or **out-of-the-box ideas**.

Example of Playful Tone:

- *"If you could wave a magic wand and solve one big problem in your industry, what would it be?"*

This prompt uses a **whimsical metaphor** to make the question less formal and more imaginative. Playful tones work well in **creative environments**, where unconventional answers are encouraged.

When to Use a Playful Tone:

- **In creative brainstorming or team-building activities**: Playful tones help participants **relax** and tap into their **imagination**.
- **In low-stakes scenarios**: When the goal is to **generate ideas** rather than find definitive solutions, playful prompts can spark interesting discussions.

Impact:
Respondents are more likely to offer **creative, imaginative** answers and feel more comfortable expressing **wild** or unconventional ideas.

---

4. Inspirational or Encouraging Tone

An **inspirational tone** motivates the respondent by focusing on **positive** outcomes, **empowerment**, or **hope**. This tone is particularly effective when encouraging personal growth, team collaboration, or big-picture thinking.

Example of Inspirational Tone:

- *"How can we, as leaders, inspire our teams to achieve their full potential and create a work environment where everyone thrives?"*

This tone invites the respondent to think about **possibilities** and **positive outcomes**. It suggests that the task at hand is both important and achievable, motivating the respondent to approach the question with **optimism**.

When to Use an Inspirational Tone:

- **In leadership discussions or goal-setting prompts**: This tone encourages respondents to focus on **aspiration** and **motivation**, helping them think about **how to achieve success**.
- **In personal development or team-building activities**: An inspirational tone creates a **supportive** atmosphere, helping people reflect on **growth** and **potential**.

Impact:
Respondents are more likely to feel **motivated** and offer **optimistic, forward-thinking** solutions.

---

5. Analytical or Objective Tone

An **analytical tone** asks the respondent to focus on **logic, data**, and **evidence**. It's best suited for situations where critical thinking is required, such as when evaluating information or solving complex problems.

Example of Analytical Tone:

- *"What are the potential economic consequences of implementing this policy, and how do they compare to similar policies introduced in other regions?"*

Here, the tone is **neutral** and **data-driven**, encouraging the respondent to rely on **facts, comparisons,** and **analytical reasoning**. This tone helps keep the response focused on **objective analysis** rather than personal opinion.

When to Use an Analytical Tone:

- **In problem-solving or decision-making prompts**: This tone encourages respondents to focus on **logic** and **critical evaluation** rather than emotions or intuition.
- **In academic or technical contexts**: Analytical tones are perfect when you need respondents to **back up their claims** with data or research.

Impact:
Respondents are likely to provide **detailed, evidence-based** responses that focus on **analysis** rather than subjective input.

Choosing the Right Tone for Your Audience

The **audience** plays a critical role in determining which tone is appropriate. Understanding the background, expectations, and goals of your audience ensures that the tone of your prompt aligns with the way they are likely to respond.

For example:

- A **senior management team** might prefer a more formal and analytical tone to ensure responses are grounded in **evidence** and focus on **strategic outcomes**.
- A **team of creatives** in a brainstorming session would likely respond better to a playful, conversational tone that invites them to explore **imaginative ideas** without constraints.

How to Control Tone in Prompt Design

Here are some simple strategies to control tone and match it to the desired response:

1. **Use Personal Pronouns to Soften the Tone**:
   Personal pronouns like "you" and "your" make the tone more **relaxed** and **inclusive**.
   Example:

   ○ Formal: *"What are the challenges of remote work?"*
   ○ Conversational: *"What challenges have you experienced with remote work, and how did you overcome them?"*

2. **Adjust Sentence Structure**:
   Longer, more complex sentences tend to create a more **formal** tone, while shorter, more straightforward sentences result in a more **informal** tone.

3. **Incorporate Emotional or Value-Laden Language**:
   Words like **inspire**, **thrive**, and **challenge** can invoke an **emotional response** and encourage more **passionate** or **reflective** answers.

4. **umor or Imagination to Create Playfulness**:
   Introducing whimsical or imaginative elements can lighten the tone and make the prompt feel more **approachable** and **fun**.
   Example:

   ○ Serious: *"What are the main obstacles to innovation in your field?"*
   ○ Playful: *"If you could remove one obstacle to innovation with the wave of a magic wand, what would it be and why?"*

5. **Adjust Vocabulary for the Desired Level of Formality**:
   Formal tone often requires more precise and sophisticated vocabulary, while informal tone relies on simpler, more conversational words.
   Example:

   ○ Formal: *"What are the primary mechanisms driving market disruption in the financial sector?"*
   ○ Conversational: *"What do you think is shaking up the financial world right now?"*

The Subtle Influence of Tone on Depth and Detail

Tone not only sets the emotional mood of the response but can also subtly influence the **depth** and **detail** of the answer. A formal, analytical tone often encourages more **structured, detailed** answers, while a playful tone may invite **broader**, more **imaginative** responses.

Example:

- **Formal/Analytical:**
"Please provide an in-depth analysis of the key factors contributing to employee disengagement in remote work environments, using recent studies as supporting evidence."
➡ The tone invites a response that is **thorough, fact-based**, and **supported by research**.
- **Conversational/Creative:**
"What's one surprising way remote work has changed your day-to-day life? How do you think this change will affect how we work in the future?"
➡ The tone is **personal** and **reflective**, encouraging respondents to share more subjective, **speculative** insights.

When crafting prompts, you can adjust the tone to control how **in-depth** or **imaginative** the responses are likely to be.

Conclusion: Using Tone as a Tool

Tone is an often-underestimated tool in prompt engineering, but it's essential for guiding the **emotional engagement, depth**, and **creativity** of responses. By thoughtfully adjusting the tone of your prompts, you can influence the way respondents interpret and answer your questions, whether you're looking for structured analyses, creative brainstorming, or personal reflection.

Tone is flexible, and by experimenting with different styles, you can ensure your prompts are perfectly aligned with your goals and audience. Whether you need seriousness or spontaneity, precision or playfulness, tone helps you create the right **atmosphere** for thoughtful and engaging responses.

In the next chapter, we'll dive into **visual imagery** and how using descriptive language in prompts can enhance clarity, creativity, and depth of responses.

CHAPTER 9: VISUAL IMAGERY – USING DESCRIPTIVE LANGUAGE FOR CLARITY

Words have the power to paint vivid pictures in our minds, and when crafting prompts, using **descriptive language** can unlock creativity, enhance clarity, and stimulate deeper responses. By incorporating **visual imagery**, you can make abstract ideas more concrete, guide the respondent's imagination, and elicit more detailed and thoughtful answers.

In this chapter, we'll explore how to use visual imagery in your prompts, the impact it has on clarity and engagement, and how descriptive language helps craft prompts that lead to richer, more nuanced responses.

The Power of Visual Imagery in Prompts

Visual imagery involves using **descriptive language** to help the respondent **see** the situation more clearly, turning abstract concepts into something more **tangible**. When a respondent can vividly imagine a scenario, they are more likely to engage deeply with the prompt and respond with **greater detail** and **creativity**.

Consider this comparison:

1. *"What is the future of transportation?"*
2. *"Imagine a future where self-driving cars zip silently through the streets, flying drones deliver packages to doorsteps, and*

high-speed trains connect cities in minutes. How might these innovations reshape urban life?"

In the second prompt, visual imagery makes the question more **engaging** and **specific**. It invites the respondent to **visualize** a futuristic world, which can spark a more creative and thoughtful response.

How Descriptive Language Enhances Clarity

When you use visual imagery, you create **clarity** by helping respondents grasp complex or abstract concepts more easily. **Concrete descriptions** give respondents a better understanding of what you're asking, allowing them to engage with the prompt on a deeper level.

Example:

- **Vague Prompt**: *"How can we improve urban spaces?"*
- **Descriptive Prompt**: *"Picture a bustling city park filled with greenery, where cyclists glide along tree-lined paths, and children play in vibrant, open spaces. What steps can we take to create more inviting urban environments like this?"*

In the second version, the prompt is no longer an abstract question about urban spaces. It's a vivid **scene** that helps the respondent imagine the type of environment you're asking them to consider. This additional clarity guides the respondent toward a **specific** and **engaging** answer.

Techniques for Using Visual Imagery in Prompts

To harness the power of descriptive language and visual imagery, consider these techniques when crafting prompts:

---

1. Paint a Picture with Your Words

When creating a prompt, use **specific details** that help the respondent visualize the scene or concept you're describing. By painting a mental picture, you give the respondent something **tangible** to work with.

Example:

- **Basic Prompt**: *"How might technology change the classroom of the future?"*
- **Descriptive Prompt**: *"Imagine stepping into a classroom of the future, where holographic displays project immersive lessons, AI tutors offer personalized feedback, and students collaborate through virtual reality. How will these technologies reshape education?"*

Here, the visual elements—**holographic displays, AI tutors, virtual reality**—bring the concept of future classrooms to life. This makes it easier for the respondent to picture the scenario and dive into a more **thoughtful** response.

---

2. Use Sensory Language

Sensory language engages the reader's **senses**—sight, sound, touch, taste, and smell. Incorporating sensory details helps respondents immerse themselves in the scene, which can lead to richer, more imaginative answers.

Example:

- **Without Sensory Detail**: *"What's your ideal work environment?"*
- **With Sensory Detail**: *"Imagine your ideal work environment— sunlight streaming through large windows, the soft hum of distant conversation, the scent of fresh coffee brewing nearby. What makes this space perfect for productivity and creativity?"*

The sensory details (sunlight, sound, scent) give the respondent more **cues** to work with, leading to a more vivid and **personalized** response.

---

3. Use Metaphors and Similes

Metaphors and similes are powerful tools for making abstract concepts more **relatable** by comparing them to something familiar. These comparisons help respondents grasp complex ideas more easily, and they often evoke more **emotional** or **creative** responses.

Example:

- **Without Metaphor**: *"How do you approach problem-solving in your work?"*
- **With Metaphor**: *"When you encounter a challenge at work, do you approach it like a chess player, strategizing every move, or like a mountain climber, tackling each obstacle as it comes? How does your approach help you overcome obstacles?"*

By comparing problem-solving to **chess** and **mountain climbing**, the second prompt helps respondents understand different strategies in a **relatable** way. Metaphors and similes stimulate **imagination** and encourage respondents to think about the question from new angles.

---

4. Use Active, Dynamic Language

Active language brings your prompts to life by using **verbs** and **adjectives** that convey movement, change, or action. This kind of language helps the respondent feel more **involved** in the scenario, prompting them to consider it with greater **engagement**.

Example:

- **Static Prompt**: *"What might cities look like in the future?"*
- **Dynamic Prompt**: *"Picture cities of the future, where electric cars glide silently through streets, vertical gardens bloom on towering skyscrapers, and smart technology adjusts energy use in real time. How will these advancements shape urban life?"*

The use of **dynamic verbs** like glide, bloom, and adjust creates a sense of **movement** and **change**, making the scenario feel more real and compelling.

5. Create Contrast to Highlight Key Ideas

By contrasting two different scenarios or concepts, you help respondents see things more clearly. Contrast emphasizes **differences**, prompting respondents to think more deeply about the nuances of the question.

Example:

- **Without Contrast**: *"What's the impact of technology on communication?"*
- **With Contrast**: *"Consider how communication has evolved— from handwritten letters that took days to arrive, to instant messaging that happens in the blink of an eye. How has this shift changed the way we connect with others?"*

The contrast between **slow, deliberate letters** and **instant messaging** highlights the **radical transformation** in communication, encouraging respondents to explore the impact in greater depth.

Balancing Visual Imagery with Clarity

While visual imagery enhances prompts, it's important not to overload the respondent with too many details or overly complex descriptions. The goal is to **enhance clarity**, not obscure it. Keep your imagery **focused** and **relevant** to the question at hand, ensuring that it helps guide the respondent rather than overwhelm them.

Example of Overloaded Imagery:

- *"Imagine a bustling city of the future, where solar-powered drones whiz overhead, electric buses glide silently through streets lined with eco-friendly skyscrapers covered in vertical gardens, and smart grids optimize energy use while autonomous delivery robots roam the sidewalks. How will these changes impact daily life?"*

While this prompt is visually rich, it might be **too detailed**, making it harder for the respondent to focus on answering the question.

Instead, simplify the imagery to guide the respondent without overloading their senses.

Revised Example:

- *"Imagine a city where smart technology and clean energy work together to create efficient, sustainable urban spaces. How might these changes affect the way people live and work?"*

This version retains **visual impact** while being more **focused** and easier for the respondent to engage with.

How Visual Imagery Encourages Deeper Responses

By creating a vivid mental image, you help respondents become more **immersed** in the scenario, making it easier for them to explore **deeper connections** and provide more **thoughtful** answers. Visual imagery makes the prompt feel more **real**, encouraging respondents to engage with it on a more **personal** level.

Example:

- Without imagery: *"How can we improve our city's transportation system?"*
- With imagery: *"Picture a city where public transportation is seamless, with trains and buses arriving exactly when needed, and bicycle lanes stretching from one side of the city to the other. How can we make this vision a reality in our city's transportation system?"*

The second prompt invites the respondent to think more deeply by **immersing** them in the scenario, encouraging them to explore specific steps toward improvement.

Conclusion: Harnessing Visual Imagery for Better Prompts

Visual imagery is a powerful tool that transforms simple prompts into **engaging, thought-provoking** questions. By using descriptive language, sensory details, metaphors, and dynamic language, you can guide respondents to **visualize** the scenario more clearly, resulting in richer, more detailed responses. The key is to strike the right balance—using imagery to **enhance** clarity without overwhelming the respondent.

In the next chapter, we'll explore the concept of **iterative refinement**, showing how prompts can evolve through continuous adjustments to achieve more focused, high-quality responses.

CHAPTER 10: ITERATIVE REFINEMENT – EVOLVING YOUR PROMPTS

Crafting a great prompt isn't always a one-time process. The best prompts are often the result of **iterative refinement**, where adjustments and tweaks lead to more **precise, engaging,** and **effective** questions. Refining prompts is a powerful way to ensure that they align with your goals, generate the responses you're looking for, and continue to evolve based on feedback and outcomes.

In this chapter, we'll explore the concept of iterative refinement, the steps to evolve your prompts through continuous adjustments, and how this approach leads to more focused and high-quality responses over time.

The Concept of Iterative Refinement

Iterative refinement is the process of improving a prompt through a series of adjustments. Instead of viewing a prompt as static or final, this method sees each version of the prompt as a **work in progress**—one that can be fine-tuned to better meet the desired outcomes. Through iteration, you can continually enhance the clarity, depth, and focus of your prompts.

Consider how the following prompt evolves over a series of refinements:

1. **Initial Prompt**: *"How can we improve company culture?"*

2. **First Iteration**: *"What are the key factors that influence company culture, and how can we enhance them to create a more positive work environment?"*
3. **Second Iteration**: *"How can we improve communication and team engagement to foster a more collaborative and inclusive company culture?"*
4. **Final Iteration**: *"What specific communication practices and team-building activities can we implement to enhance collaboration and inclusivity in our company culture?"*

With each version, the prompt becomes more **focused** and **actionable**, evolving from a broad, general question to a more specific and effective one.

Why Refinement is Necessary

No matter how well-crafted a prompt may seem at first, there is always room for improvement. Through refinement, you can address several key areas:

1. **Clarity**: Is the question clear and easy to understand? Does it avoid confusion or vagueness?
2. **Focus**: Does the prompt lead the respondent to the specific type of answer you're seeking, or is it too broad?
3. **Depth**: Does the prompt encourage deeper thinking and exploration, or is the response likely to be superficial?
4. **Relevance**: Does the prompt align with the context and audience? Does it fit the goals of the conversation or project?

Refining prompts ensures that they are **tailored, focused,** and designed to generate the most **meaningful** responses possible.

Steps to Iterative Refinement

Here's a step-by-step process to refine your prompts iteratively, ensuring continuous improvement and alignment with your goals.

Step 1: Assess the Initial Version

Start by creating the initial version of the prompt. This first draft doesn't need to be perfect—it simply needs to capture the essence of what you're asking. Once you have the initial version, **assess** it against key criteria such as:

- **Does it convey the right message?**
- **Is it too broad or too specific?**
- **What type of responses is it likely to generate?**

Example:
Initial Prompt: *"How can we innovate more effectively as a team?"*

Assessment:

- The question is clear, but it may be too **broad**.
- It doesn't specify what area of innovation (process, product, or communication).
- The respondent might struggle to know where to focus their answer.

Step 2: Identify Areas for Improvement

After assessing the prompt, identify specific areas that need refinement. Ask yourself:

- **Should the prompt be narrowed down or expanded?**
- **Are there terms or phrases that need to be clarified?**
- **Is the question guiding the respondent toward a meaningful response?**

Example:
For the initial prompt, you might decide that "innovation" is too broad and that the prompt needs to focus on a **specific aspect** of team innovation, such as collaboration or process improvement.

Step 3: Make Focused Adjustments

Once you've identified the areas for improvement, make focused adjustments to the prompt. Consider making the question more specific or clarifying ambiguous terms.

Example:
Refined Prompt: *"How can we improve our team's collaboration to foster more effective innovation?"*

This version adds specificity by focusing on **team collaboration**, making it clearer where the respondent should direct their thoughts.

Step 4: Test the Prompt with Respondents

Before settling on a final version, **test** the refined prompt with a small group of respondents or in a controlled environment. Collect feedback on how well the prompt performs:

- **Were the responses insightful and relevant?**
- **Did the respondents understand the question clearly?**
- **Were there any patterns in the answers that suggest further refinement is needed?**

By testing the prompt, you can gather valuable insights on its effectiveness and identify any **unintended issues** that may have surfaced.

Step 5: Refine Based on Feedback

After testing, gather the feedback and refine the prompt further. Pay attention to any issues with **clarity**, **focus**, or **engagement**, and make additional tweaks as needed.

Example:
Feedback from the test group might suggest that "collaboration" is still too broad. As a result, you refine the prompt further:

- *"How can we improve our team's communication and idea-sharing processes to foster more effective innovation?"*

This final iteration breaks down collaboration into **specific processes**—communication and idea-sharing—making the prompt clearer and more actionable.

Step 6: Repeat the Process as Needed

Iterative refinement is a **cyclical** process. If necessary, continue refining the prompt based on additional feedback or new insights. Over time, each iteration will bring you closer to a prompt that generates the desired results.

Examples of Iterative Refinement in Action

Let's walk through a couple of examples to see how iterative refinement can improve prompts.

Example 1: Problem-Solving in Education

1. **Initial Prompt**:
   "How can we improve student learning in the classroom?"
   Assessment:

   o   The prompt is clear but too broad. "Student learning" could mean anything from academic performance to engagement or emotional well-being.

2. **First Iteration**:
   "What strategies can we implement to improve student engagement in the classroom?"
   Improvement:

   o   This version focuses on **engagement**, which gives respondents a clearer focus but is still fairly open-ended.

3. **Second Iteration**:
   "How can we use interactive technologies to increase student

engagement in STEM subjects in the classroom?"
Improvement:

o   This version specifies **interactive technologies** and **STEM subjects**, narrowing the focus and ensuring responses are more targeted.

Example 2: Leadership Development

1. **Initial Prompt**:
   "How can leaders improve employee motivation?"
   Assessment:

o   The prompt is vague and doesn't provide much direction for respondents. "Motivation" could mean many things.

2. **First Iteration**:
   "What strategies can leaders use to motivate employees in high-stress work environments?"
   Improvement:

o   Adding **high-stress environments** makes the prompt more specific, but it could still benefit from additional focus.

3. **Second Iteration**:
   "What specific leadership practices can we implement to motivate employees in high-stress work environments, while promoting work-life balance and mental well-being?"
   Improvement:

o   This version incorporates **leadership practices, work-life balance**, and **mental well-being**, encouraging deeper responses that address multiple facets of employee motivation.

The Benefits of Iterative Refinement

Refining prompts iteratively offers several key benefits:

1. **Improved Clarity**: Through refinement, you remove ambiguity and ensure that the prompt is easy to understand.
2. **Greater Focus**: Each iteration narrows the scope, helping respondents provide answers that are relevant and aligned with your goals.
3. **More Depth**: As prompts become more refined, they encourage deeper, more thoughtful responses that explore complex issues.
4. **Better Alignment**: Iterative refinement ensures that the prompt is **tailored** to the specific audience and context, increasing the likelihood of meaningful engagement.

Conclusion: Embracing Iterative Refinement

Prompt design is rarely perfect on the first attempt. Iterative refinement is a powerful tool that allows you to continuously improve your prompts, ensuring they evolve to better meet your needs and generate more valuable responses. By assessing, adjusting, and refining your prompts over time, you can create questions that are clearer, more focused, and more engaging.

In the next chapter, we'll explore the use of **examples in prompts** and how offering specific models or cases can guide respondents without limiting their creativity.

CHAPTER 11: LEVERAGING EXAMPLES – GUIDING WITHOUT DICTATING

Using examples in prompts can serve as a powerful tool to provide clarity, inspire creativity, and guide respondents toward specific types of answers—without limiting their freedom to explore different perspectives. By incorporating examples, you can help respondents better understand the context or direction you're aiming for, while still leaving room for **interpretation** and **originality**.

In this chapter, we'll explore how to use examples effectively in prompt design, the benefits of providing clear models, and how to strike a balance between guiding responses and fostering creativity.

Why Use Examples in Prompts?

Examples serve as a **frame of reference** for respondents, giving them a concrete starting point to base their answers on. When used correctly, examples can:

- **Clarify expectations**: Offering a model helps respondents understand the scope of the prompt, making it easier to provide relevant and meaningful answers.
- **Spark creativity**: Examples can inspire new ideas by showing possibilities that respondents may not have thought of.
- **Reduce confusion**: By providing a concrete case or scenario, you can remove ambiguity from the prompt, helping respondents focus on what matters most.

For example:

- Without example: *"What strategies can we use to improve team collaboration?"*
- With example: *"What strategies, such as daily stand-up meetings or collaborative project management tools, can we use to improve team collaboration?"*

The version with examples gives respondents **specific ideas** of what strategies to think about (daily stand-up meetings, project management tools), helping them narrow their focus without dictating a single "right" answer.

When to Use Examples in Prompts

Examples can be used effectively in a variety of contexts, including:

1. **Explaining Complex Concepts**: When a topic is abstract or complicated, examples provide a concrete way to clarify what the prompt is asking for.
2. **Providing Direction**: If the prompt is broad, examples can help respondents understand the kinds of answers you're looking for.
3. **Inspiring Creativity**: In brainstorming or idea-generation prompts, examples can serve as a springboard for creativity by showing respondents what's possible.
4. **Reducing Ambiguity**: When there's potential for the prompt to be interpreted in too many different ways, examples can help focus responses.

Example:

- Without example: *"How can we use technology to improve customer service?"*
- With example: *"How can we use technology, such as chatbots, mobile apps, or AI-powered help desks, to improve customer service?"*

By providing examples (chatbots, mobile apps, AI-powered help desks), the second version gives respondents a clearer sense of what kind of technologies they might consider, while still allowing them to explore other possibilities.

The Benefits of Using Examples in Prompts

Let's look at the specific benefits that come from using examples in prompt design.

1. Clarifying Ambiguous Concepts

When a prompt deals with an abstract or unfamiliar concept, examples can make it easier for respondents to understand what you're asking for. By providing a specific case or model, you help respondents grasp the idea without needing lengthy explanations.

Example:

- Without example: *"What are some ways to increase innovation in the workplace?"*
- With example: *"What are some ways to increase innovation in the workplace, such as hackathons, cross-departmental brainstorming sessions, or employee idea submission platforms?"*

In the second version, the examples clarify what types of strategies might qualify as "increasing innovation," helping respondents focus on relevant approaches.

2. Inspiring Creativity by Offering a Starting Point

Examples can also help spark creativity by providing a **jumping-off point** for respondents to build upon. Rather than narrowing the scope of responses, examples can actually open the door to new ideas by giving respondents inspiration for their own unique answers.

Example:

- Without example: *"What new product ideas could we develop to meet customer needs?"*
- With example: *"What new product ideas could we develop to meet customer needs? For example, consider products that incorporate eco-friendly materials, offer subscription-based services, or enhance digital experiences."*

The second version offers a range of **starting points** for the respondent, giving them ideas to work with (eco-friendly materials, subscription-based services, digital experiences) that may inspire further innovation.

---

3. Focusing Responses Without Limiting Creativity

One of the main advantages of using examples in prompts is that they help focus responses while still leaving room for creativity. By providing a model, you give respondents a clearer idea of what's expected, but they are still free to explore alternative answers.

Example:

- Without example: *"What strategies should we use to improve employee engagement?"*
- With example: *"What strategies should we use to improve employee engagement? For instance, would implementing flexible work hours, introducing peer recognition programs, or organizing team-building retreats be effective?"*

The version with examples gives respondents clear suggestions for engagement strategies, but it doesn't **dictate** a specific solution, leaving room for creativity and additional ideas.

---

4. Encouraging Depth in Responses

Examples encourage respondents to dive deeper into their answers by giving them **something to compare or contrast**. Rather than providing a surface-level response, respondents are prompted to explore the nuances of the example and expand upon it.

Example:

- Without example: *"How can businesses implement more sustainable practices?"*
- With example: *"How can businesses implement more sustainable practices? For example, what role could renewable energy, waste reduction initiatives, or supply chain transparency play in achieving sustainability goals?"*

The second version with examples encourages respondents to **dig deeper** into specific sustainability practices, prompting them to think about how each example (renewable energy, waste reduction, supply chain transparency) could be applied in a business context.

Balancing Guidance with Flexibility

The challenge with using examples is finding the right balance between **guiding** the respondent and **allowing creative freedom**. While examples provide clarity and focus, they should not feel like they are **restricting** the respondent to a single path or answer.

Here's how to balance guidance with flexibility when using examples in prompts:

---

1. Offer Multiple Examples to Show Variety

Rather than giving just one example, provide **multiple options** to illustrate a range of possibilities. This demonstrates that there are many valid approaches, encouraging respondents to think outside the box.

Example:

- Narrow: *"What benefits could we offer to attract top talent? For example, flexible work hours."*
- Expanded: *"What benefits could we offer to attract top talent? For instance, consider offering flexible work hours, professional development opportunities, or wellness programs."*

By providing multiple examples, the second version encourages respondents to explore different options while avoiding the feeling of being boxed in by a single idea.

---

2. Use Examples as Inspiration, Not a Blueprint

Make it clear that the examples you provide are meant to **inspire** respondents, not limit their creativity. You can use language like "for example" or "such as" to show that the examples are merely **suggestions**, not strict guidelines.

Example:

- **Restrictive**: *"What are the best ways to market our product using social media ads?"*
- **Flexible**: *"What are the best ways to market our product? For example, consider using social media ads, influencer partnerships, or content marketing strategies."*

In the flexible version, respondents are invited to **consider different options**, but they aren't limited to just the examples provided.

---

3. Encourage Respondents to Build on the Example

Another way to balance guidance and flexibility is to **encourage respondents** to expand on or improve the example. This invites them to think critically about the example and explore ways to **enhance** or **adapt** it.

Example:

- Without expansion: *"How can we improve customer satisfaction with our services?"*
- With expansion: *"How can we improve customer satisfaction with our services? For example, how could a more personalized customer support experience, faster response times, or loyalty rewards improve satisfaction?"*

In this version, the examples not only offer ideas but also encourage the respondent to think about **how they might improve or build upon** those ideas.

Examples in Action: How to Leverage Them Effectively

Let's look at a few different examples to see how they can be used effectively in prompt design.

Example 1: Promoting Innovation

1. **Without Example**:
   "How can we drive more innovation in our product development process?"
2. **With Example**:
   "How can we drive more innovation in our product development process? For example, would organizing cross-functional innovation workshops or adopting rapid prototyping methods help?"

Impact:
The second version offers **specific strategies** (innovation workshops, rapid prototyping), helping respondents focus on practical approaches to innovation while still leaving room for creative alternatives.

Example 2: Brainstorming Marketing Ideas

1. **Without Example**:
   "What are some creative ways we can market our new product?"
2. **With Example**:
   "What are some creative ways we can market our new product? Consider using influencer marketing, interactive social media campaigns, or experiential events to create buzz."

Impact:
The examples of **influencer marketing, interactive campaigns**, and **experiential events** give respondents a **jumping-off point**, inspiring more creative and diverse marketing strategies.

Conclusion: Guiding Without Dictating

Examples are a valuable tool in prompt design,helping to **guide** respondents toward meaningful answers without **dictating** their responses. By offering clear models, you can clarify complex ideas, inspire creativity, and focus responses, while still allowing room for **interpretation** and **originality**. The key is to use examples in a way that **opens up possibilities**, not restricts them, by offering multiple options, encouraging expansion, and presenting examples as suggestions rather than rules.

In the next chapter, we'll explore the concept of **indirect guidance**, where subtle cues and suggestions can steer responses without giving explicit instructions.

CHAPTER 12: INDIRECT GUIDANCE – SUBTLE STEERING THROUGH SUGGESTION

In prompt engineering, the most effective guidance isn't always overt. Sometimes, the best way to steer a response is through **indirect guidance**, where subtle hints and suggestions lead the respondent toward deeper, more thoughtful answers without them feeling overtly directed. This chapter will focus on how to nudge respondents toward specific outcomes or ideas by employing **subtle cues**, offering **gentle constraints**, and framing prompts in ways that inspire the kind of answers you want without explicitly dictating them.

What is Indirect Guidance?

Indirect guidance involves shaping the respondent's thinking through subtle suggestions embedded within the prompt. Rather than outright telling the respondent what to focus on or how to answer, you **steer** them in the right direction by:

- **Framing the question** in a way that emphasizes particular aspects.
- **Implying constraints** or limitations that naturally guide the response.
- **Using hints or leading phrases** that suggest certain types of answers without explicitly stating them.

This approach preserves the **freedom** of the respondent while helping them avoid wandering too far from the key themes or objectives of the prompt.

Why Use Indirect Guidance?

Indirect guidance is particularly useful when:

- You want to avoid **leading** the respondent too forcefully, allowing them to think independently but still within certain boundaries.
- The subject matter requires a more **exploratory** or creative approach, but you want to keep responses **relevant**.
- You're looking for nuanced, layered responses that touch on certain **themes** without forcing a particular answer.

For example:

- **Direct Prompt**: *"What are the environmental benefits of renewable energy?"*
- **Indirect Prompt**: *"How might renewable energy sources, such as solar and wind, reduce the strain on natural resources and decrease pollution?"*

In the second version, the respondent is subtly led to consider **resource conservation** and **pollution reduction** as key environmental benefits, but the phrasing still leaves room for exploration.

Techniques for Indirect Guidance

Here are some key techniques for steering responses subtly while maintaining the respondent's sense of independence.

1. Framing the Question with Implied Focus

One of the simplest ways to guide respondents indirectly is by **framing** the prompt in such a way that it naturally emphasizes certain aspects of the topic. By hinting at a particular angle, you encourage respondents to explore it more deeply without directly instructing them to do so.

Example:

- **Direct**: *"What are the pros and cons of remote work?"*
- **Indirect**: *"As remote work becomes more common, how might it reshape productivity, employee satisfaction, and collaboration within teams?"*

In the indirect version, you guide the respondent to focus on **productivity**, **satisfaction**, and **collaboration** by including these as natural areas of consideration within the prompt.

---

2. Use Leading Phrases to Encourage Exploration

Leading phrases can gently nudge the respondent toward the type of response you're looking for. Words like "in what ways," "how might," and "consider" invite the respondent to explore specific themes without feeling constrained.

Example:

- **Direct**: *"How can we improve our company's diversity policies?"*
- **Indirect**: *"In what ways might we create more inclusive hiring practices that lead to a more diverse workforce?"*

The phrase "in what ways" signals to the respondent that you're asking for **methods** or **strategies** rather than just general statements, and the focus on **hiring practices** narrows the scope while still leaving room for different ideas.

---

3. Introduce Gentle Constraints Through Context

Introducing subtle constraints in your prompt helps respondents stay within a certain framework, guiding them without making them feel restricted. This can be done by adding a specific **context** or **hypothetical situation** that narrows the field of possibilities while still leaving room for exploration.

Example:

- **Without Constraint**: *"What are some ways to reduce business expenses?"*
- **With Constraint**: *"Given the current shift toward remote work, how might companies reduce office-related expenses without sacrificing employee productivity?"*

In the second version, the context of remote work provides a **constraint** that focuses the respondent's thinking on a particular area (office-related expenses), but they're still free to explore different solutions.

---

4. Suggest Themes Without Limiting Responses

You can steer respondents toward certain themes by suggesting areas they might want to explore without explicitly requiring them to do so. This allows for **independence**, but gently directs the flow of their thinking.

Example:

- **Direct**: *"What are the challenges of implementing AI in healthcare?"*
- **Indirect**: *"What are some potential challenges of implementing AI in healthcare, such as ethical concerns, data security, or patient trust?"*

The examples of **ethical concerns**, **data security**, and **patient trust** guide the respondent to consider these themes, but they can still explore other challenges if they wish.

---

5. Encourage Exploration with Open-Ended Hypotheticals

Using **hypotheticals** allows you to create scenarios that subtly steer respondents toward specific ideas while encouraging them to **imagine** and **explore**. This technique works particularly well for prompts that require creative or speculative responses.

Example:

- **Without Hypothetical**: *"How will future technologies affect education?"*
- **With Hypothetical**: *"Imagine a future where virtual reality and AI are fully integrated into education systems. How might these technologies change the way students learn and teachers interact with their classes?"*

The hypothetical scenario focuses the respondent on the impact of **VR** and **AI**, but they are still free to speculate about the broader effects on education.

The Benefits of Indirect Guidance

By using indirect guidance, you can:

1. **Encourage Thoughtful, Nuanced Responses**: When respondents are subtly guided, they are more likely to explore **multiple perspectives** and provide layered answers.
2. **Foster Independence and Creativity**: Respondents feel a greater sense of **freedom** in their thinking, leading to more **innovative** or **insightful** answers.
3. **Reduce the Risk of Surface-Level Responses**: Subtle steering helps avoid overly simplistic or broad responses by encouraging deeper exploration of specific themes.
4. **Create Balanced Responses**: Indirect guidance ensures that respondents touch on key points without feeling like they're being forced into a specific response, leading to more **balanced** and **comprehensive** answers.

Examples of Indirect Guidance in Action

Let's look at a few examples to see how indirect guidance can be used effectively in different types of prompts.

Example 1: Innovation in Business

1. **Direct Prompt**:
   "How can businesses innovate in today's competitive market?"
2. **Indirect Prompt**:
   "As competition increases, in what ways might businesses leverage technology, customer insights, or partnerships to drive innovation and stay ahead in the market?"

Impact:
The indirect version subtly directs the respondent to think about **technology**, **customer insights**, and **partnerships** without explicitly requiring them to focus on these areas, giving them flexibility to explore other options.

Example 2: Sustainability in Urban Planning

1. **Direct Prompt**:
   "What are the benefits of sustainable urban planning?"
2. **Indirect Prompt**:
   "As cities grow, how might sustainable urban planning—such as the use of green spaces, renewable energy, and public transportation—create healthier and more livable environments for future generations?"

Impact:
The indirect version hints at specific areas of focus (**green spaces, renewable energy, public transportation**) while still allowing respondents to consider other aspects of sustainable planning.

Conclusion: The Art of Subtle Steering

Indirect guidance is a powerful tool in prompt design that encourages deeper, more thoughtful responses without imposing rigid constraints. By framing questions, using leading phrases, offering gentle constraints, and suggesting themes, you can guide respondents toward certain ideas and outcomes while still allowing for **independence** and **creativity**. This balance between **guidance** and **freedom** ensures that responses are both focused and insightful.

In the next chapter, we'll explore **interdisciplinary prompts**, where concepts from different fields are blended to create more complex and nuanced questions.

CHAPTER 13: INTERDISCIPLINARY PROMPTS – BORROWING FROM THE ARTS, SCIENCES, AND MORE

Interdisciplinary prompts blend concepts, methods, and ideas from **multiple fields** to create richer, more nuanced questions. By drawing on the **arts**, **sciences**, **business**, **literature**, and other domains, you can encourage respondents to think more broadly, apply diverse perspectives, and explore connections between different disciplines.

In this chapter, we'll explore the power of interdisciplinary prompts, how to create them, and how combining fields can lead to more innovative, complex, and insightful responses.

What Are Interdisciplinary Prompts?

An interdisciplinary prompt blends knowledge or methods from two or more fields to create a question that **crosses boundaries** and encourages respondents to think beyond their usual frame of reference. This can lead to more **creative**, **thought-provoking** answers, as respondents are invited to consider how different disciplines might interact to solve problems, generate ideas, or develop new perspectives.

For example:

- **Single-discipline prompt**: *"How does artificial intelligence impact the healthcare industry?"*
- **Interdisciplinary prompt**: *"How can insights from psychology, AI, and data science be combined to improve mental health care in the next decade?"*

The second version merges psychology, AI, and data science, encouraging the respondent to think about how these fields intersect to address mental health challenges. This makes the prompt more **complex** and **multifaceted**, leading to deeper, more integrated responses.

Why Use Interdisciplinary Prompts?

Interdisciplinary prompts are particularly powerful because they:

- **Encourage innovation**: By combining fields, respondents are pushed to think creatively and explore new solutions.
- **Promote deeper thinking**: Interdisciplinary prompts challenge respondents to see connections between seemingly unrelated topics, fostering more **nuanced** thinking.
- **Reflect real-world complexity**: In the real world, problems often require solutions that span multiple disciplines. These prompts reflect that complexity, making responses more applicable and relevant.
- **Inspire collaboration**: When working in teams, interdisciplinary prompts can lead to more collaborative and diverse discussions, where different areas of expertise are shared.

How to Create Interdisciplinary Prompts

Crafting an effective interdisciplinary prompt requires blending concepts from different fields in a way that makes sense and opens up new avenues of thinking. Here are some strategies to help you design such prompts:

---

1. Identify Common Themes Across Disciplines

Look for **common themes** or questions that apply to multiple fields. For example, innovation, sustainability, ethics, or creativity are topics that can be explored from the perspectives of both the arts and sciences.

Example:

- **General prompt**: *"How can technology improve education?"*
- **Interdisciplinary prompt**: *"How can principles from both educational psychology and AI technology be used to create more personalized learning experiences for students?"*

By combining **educational psychology** with **AI technology**, this prompt invites respondents to think about how insights from both fields can be applied together to solve a problem.

---

2. Encourage Cross-Disciplinary Problem Solving

When crafting interdisciplinary prompts, challenge respondents to **solve problems** by drawing on ideas from different fields. This approach encourages creative, out-of-the-box thinking by requiring respondents to make **connections** between disciplines.

Example:

- **Single-discipline prompt**: *"What are the best ways to reduce energy consumption in cities?"*
- **Interdisciplinary prompt**: *"How can urban design, behavioral psychology, and renewable energy technologies work together to reduce energy consumption in cities?"*

Here, the prompt combines **urban design**, **psychology**, and **renewable energy technologies**, encouraging respondents to consider how each of these fields might contribute to solving the energy consumption problem.

---

3. Explore the Intersection of Arts and Sciences

Blending the **arts** with **sciences** or **technology** can lead to particularly rich interdisciplinary prompts. The arts bring creativity, expression, and human-centered thinking, while the sciences and technology offer analytical and technical perspectives.

Example:

- **Single-discipline prompt**: *"How can technology help create more engaging museum exhibits?"*
- **Interdisciplinary prompt**: *"How might insights from interactive technology and design principles from the visual arts combine to create immersive, engaging museum exhibits?"*

In this prompt, **interactive technology** and **visual arts** come together to create a more dynamic, engaging experience for museum-goers. Respondents are encouraged to think about how both disciplines influence the outcome.

---

4. Encourage Ethical and Societal Reflection

Interdisciplinary prompts are also useful for exploring the **ethical**, **cultural**, and **societal implications** of technology, science, or business. By incorporating fields like **philosophy**, **sociology**, or **cultural studies**, you invite respondents to reflect on the broader consequences of innovation.

Example:

- **Single-discipline prompt**: *"What are the risks of using AI in decision-making?"*
- **Interdisciplinary prompt**: *"How might insights from philosophy and data ethics help us navigate the risks and responsibilities of using AI in critical decision-making processes?"*

In this interdisciplinary version, respondents are prompted to think not only about the technical risks of AI but also the **ethical** considerations, combining philosophy and data ethics.

---

5. Create Hypothetical Scenarios That Blend Disciplines

Using **hypothetical scenarios** is another effective way to craft interdisciplinary prompts. These scenarios can blend different fields in a creative way, pushing respondents to explore new solutions and approaches.

Example:

- **Single-discipline prompt**: *"How can we design more efficient public transportation systems?"*
- **Interdisciplinary prompt**: *"Imagine a future city where both sustainable architecture and advanced AI systems collaborate to design and manage public transportation. How might these fields work together to create a seamless, efficient urban transit system?"*

In this scenario, respondents are encouraged to think about how **sustainable architecture** and **AI** could intersect to create innovative public transportation systems.

Examples of Interdisciplinary Prompts in Action

Let's explore a few examples to see how interdisciplinary prompts can create more complex, insightful responses.

Example 1: Health and Technology

1. **Single-discipline prompt**:
   "How can wearable technology improve health monitoring?"
2. **Interdisciplinary prompt**:
   "How can insights from behavioral psychology and wearable technology be combined to encourage healthier habits and improve long-term health monitoring?"

Impact:
The interdisciplinary prompt combines **psychology** and **technology**, encouraging respondents to think about how the fields can work together to drive behavior change and improve health outcomes.

Example 2: Environmental Sustainability

1. **Single-discipline prompt**:
   "What are some ways to reduce plastic waste?"
2. **Interdisciplinary prompt**:
   "How can principles from marine biology, materials science, and environmental economics be used to develop more effective strategies for reducing plastic waste in the oceans?"

Impact:
This interdisciplinary prompt invites respondents to consider how fields like **marine biology, materials science**, and **economics** intersect to address the environmental problem of plastic waste.

Example 3: Education and the Arts

1. **Single-discipline prompt**:
   "How can art be used to enhance student learning?"
2. **Interdisciplinary prompt**:
   "In what ways can art, cognitive science, and digital technology work together to enhance student learning, especially in subjects like math and science?"

Impact:
By blending **art, cognitive science**, and **digital technology**, this prompt encourages respondents to explore how different methods of engagement can combine to create more effective learning environments.

The Benefits of Interdisciplinary Prompts

Interdisciplinary prompts provide several key advantages:

1. **Enhanced Creativity and Innovation**: By pushing respondents to think across disciplines, interdisciplinary prompts often lead to more **innovative** and **creative** solutions.

2. **Nuanced Responses**: These prompts encourage respondents to consider multiple perspectives, resulting in **more thoughtful, complex** answers.
3. **Reflecting Real-World Challenges**: Many of today's problems—whether in science, technology, or society—require **cross-disciplinary approaches**. Interdisciplinary prompts reflect this reality and prepare respondents to think about issues in a more integrated way.
4. **Inspiring Collaboration**: For group or team exercises, interdisciplinary prompts foster **collaboration** by encouraging participants to share insights from different fields.

Conclusion: The Power of Cross-Disciplinary Thinking

Interdisciplinary prompts are a powerful tool in prompt design, offering a way to combine insights from multiple fields to generate more complex, innovative, and thoughtful responses. By blending concepts from the arts, sciences, humanities, and technology, you invite respondents to **expand their thinking**, find connections across fields, and solve problems in creative new ways.

In the next chapter, we'll explore the art of **anticipating responses**, showing how reverse-engineering your prompts can help you shape them to generate the most insightful answers.

CHAPTER 14: ANTICIPATING RESPONSES – THE ART OF REVERSE ENGINEERING

Crafting effective prompts often requires you to think ahead and **anticipate** the kind of responses you want to receive. This process, known as **reverse engineering**, involves starting with the ideal response in mind and then working backward to design the prompt that will lead to those answers. By mastering this technique, you can create prompts that are **clear**, **targeted**, and **highly effective** at generating the most insightful, relevant responses.

In this chapter, we'll explore how reverse engineering works, why it's a critical skill in prompt engineering, and the steps you can take to anticipate and shape the responses you're looking for.

What Is Reverse Engineering in Prompt Design?

Reverse engineering in prompt design means **thinking about the desired outcome first** and then crafting the prompt that will naturally guide respondents toward that outcome. Rather than simply asking a question and hoping for the best, you consider:

- **What type of answer do I want?**
- **What themes, ideas, or information should the respondent address?**
- **How can I shape the prompt to encourage that type of response?**

By thinking about the **response** before the **question**, you can better control the flow of the conversation and ensure that your prompt leads to **meaningful, focused answers**.

Why Reverse Engineering Matters

When you anticipate the responses you want, you avoid the common pitfalls of poorly designed prompts, such as:

- **Vague or irrelevant answers**: Prompts that are too open-ended can lead to answers that don't align with your goals.
- **Shallow responses**: If you don't give enough guidance, respondents might provide superficial answers that don't delve into the key issues.
- **Overly broad or unfocused responses**: When prompts lack focus, respondents may struggle to know where to begin, leading to unfocused or scattered answers.

By reverse engineering prompts, you help **direct** respondents toward the answers that will be most useful, ensuring the conversation stays on track and leads to the insights you're looking for.

The Reverse Engineering Process

Here's a step-by-step guide to reverse engineering prompts, helping you craft questions that yield targeted and thoughtful responses.

1. Define the Ideal Response

The first step in reverse engineering is to start with a clear understanding of the **ideal response** you're aiming for. Ask yourself:

- **What type of information** do I need?
- **What depth or detail** do I expect?
- **What specific themes** or topics should the respondent address?

By defining what a good response looks like, you can start to shape your prompt to guide the respondent toward that answer.

Example:

- **Desired response**: A thoughtful analysis of the **ethical implications of AI** in the workplace, including considerations of privacy, fairness, and job displacement.

---

2. Work Backward to Identify Key Themes

Once you know the type of response you want, identify the **key themes** or **topics** the respondent needs to address to arrive at that response. This helps you structure your prompt in a way that naturally encourages the respondent to think about those themes.

Example:

- **Key themes**: Privacy, fairness, job displacement, and societal impact of AI in the workplace.

---

3. Shape the Prompt to Include Relevant Cues

Now that you've identified the key themes, shape the prompt so that it includes **subtle cues** or hints that will lead the respondent to address those themes. These cues can be direct or indirect, depending on the tone and style of the prompt, but they should point the respondent toward the areas you want them to explore.

Example:

- **Direct cues**: *"What are the ethical implications of AI in the workplace, particularly in terms of privacy, fairness, and job displacement?"*
- **Indirect cues**: *"As AI becomes more prevalent in the workplace, what ethical challenges might arise related to employee rights, job security, and the protection of personal data?"*

In both examples, the prompt leads the respondent to consider the themes you've identified, but in a way that feels **natural** and **open-ended**.

---

4. Consider the Depth of the Response

The way you frame your prompt can significantly impact the **depth** of the response you receive. If you want a more detailed, thoughtful answer, make sure your prompt encourages **critical thinking** and **analysis**, rather than a simple or brief reply.

To achieve depth:

- **Ask for explanations or reasoning**: Use phrases like "Explain how…" or "In what ways…"
- **Encourage comparison or contrast**: Phrases like "Compare the benefits and challenges…" invite more nuanced answers.
- **Prompt for multiple perspectives**: Ask respondents to consider different angles or viewpoints on the topic.

Example:

- Basic: *"What are the ethical challenges of AI in the workplace?"*
- Enhanced for depth: *"How might the implementation of AI in the workplace raise ethical challenges, particularly concerning privacy, fairness, and job displacement? How can companies address these challenges while still embracing technological advancement?"*

In the enhanced version, the prompt pushes for a **more thoughtful** response by encouraging the respondent to **explain the challenges** and **consider solutions**.

---

5. Test and Refine the Prompt

Once you've crafted your prompt, it's important to **test** it. Whether you're testing the prompt with colleagues, in a controlled group, or in an actual conversation, pay attention to the **quality of the responses** it generates. Are respondents addressing the key themes? Is the depth of the answer sufficient? Are the responses aligned with your goals?

If the responses are **off-target** or **too shallow**, revisit the prompt and refine it based on the feedback you've received. Adjust wording, add or remove cues, or reframe the question until the prompt consistently produces the types of responses you're aiming for.

Example:

- If the initial responses focus too much on job displacement but overlook privacy concerns, you might refine the prompt to more explicitly call attention to privacy:
"In what ways might the rise of AI in the workplace challenge employee privacy, fairness in decision-making, and the potential for job displacement?"

Anticipating Common Pitfalls

Even with careful reverse engineering, there are some common pitfalls you should watch out for when anticipating responses. Being aware of these will help you fine-tune your prompts to ensure they lead to useful answers.

---

1. Overly Narrow Responses

If your prompt is too **specific**, it may lead to overly narrow responses, leaving out important aspects. While focus is important, you don't want to overly restrict the respondent's thinking.

Solution: Balance specificity with **openness**, allowing for a range of ideas while still guiding the respondent toward key themes.

Example:

- **Overly narrow**: *"What privacy concerns should companies consider when implementing AI in the workplace?"*
➡ While this is a good question, it limits the respondent to **privacy** concerns only.
- **Refined**: *"What privacy, fairness, and job displacement concerns should companies consider when implementing AI in the*

workplace?"

➡ This broader question allows the respondent to explore multiple key areas.

---

2. Overly Broad Responses

On the flip side, if your prompt is too **vague**, you may receive broad or unfocused responses that lack the depth or specificity you're looking for.

Solution: Add **clarifying cues** or ask respondents to focus on specific aspects of the topic, ensuring that their answers stay relevant and on point.

Example:

- **Overly broad**: *"How can AI affect the workplace?"*
➡ This question is too open-ended, leading to a range of possible answers that may not be focused.
- **Refined**: *"How might AI change the way decisions are made in the workplace, and what ethical challenges could arise from this?"*
➡ This version directs the respondent to think about **decision-making** and **ethical challenges**, narrowing the scope without limiting creativity.

---

3. Shallow Responses

If respondents consistently provide **shallow** or superficial answers, it may be a sign that your prompt isn't encouraging deep enough thinking.

Solution: Rework your prompt to invite **critical thinking** by asking for explanations, justifications, or comparisons.

Example:

- **Shallow prompt**: *"How can AI improve workplace efficiency?"*
➡ Respondents might simply list surface-level benefits like speed or cost savings.

- **Enhanced prompt**: *"In what ways can AI improve workplace efficiency, and what trade-offs might companies face in terms of employee engagement and decision-making transparency?"*

➡ This version encourages respondents to explore **trade-offs** and think more critically about the broader implications of AI on efficiency.

Conclusion: Crafting Prompts with the End in Mind

Reverse engineering your prompts is an essential skill for ensuring that your questions lead to the most insightful, relevant, and thoughtful responses. By starting with the **desired outcome** in mind, identifying key themes, and shaping your prompt to encourage depth and clarity, you can anticipate the responses you need and design prompts that generate **meaningful engagement**.

In the next chapter, we'll explore the idea of **iterative dialogue**—how to create a conversation where prompts build on each other to deepen understanding and uncover complex insights.

CHAPTER 15: ITERATIVE DIALOGUE – BUILDING CONVERSATIONS OVER TIME

Creating a single, well-crafted prompt can spark insightful responses, but to truly **deepen understanding** and **uncover complex insights**, you need to develop a strategy for **iterative dialogue**. This involves crafting a series of interconnected prompts that gradually build upon one another, creating a dynamic conversation that evolves over time. Iterative dialogue allows for exploration of ideas in greater depth, encourages respondents to reflect on their previous answers, and ultimately leads to more nuanced and sophisticated responses.

In this chapter, we'll explore how to design prompts that flow naturally into one another, how to use iterative questioning to encourage deeper thinking, and how to create conversations that evolve and adapt based on responses.

What Is Iterative Dialogue?

Iterative dialogue refers to a process in which **prompts build on one another** in a sequence, forming a conversational arc that progressively uncovers deeper insights or explores different facets of a topic. Instead of relying on a single prompt to extract a complete answer, you guide the respondent through **multiple layers of inquiry**, where each prompt:

- **Reflects on previous answers**.
- **Expands or narrows focus** based on earlier responses.
- **Explores new angles** or perspectives.

This method encourages a more **interactive, thought-provoking** exchange, as respondents are given the opportunity to revisit and refine their ideas, make connections between different points, and address new questions as they emerge.

Why Use Iterative Dialogue?

In a real-world conversation, meaningful dialogue often unfolds through **follow-up questions, clarifications**, and **reflections**. Iterative prompts mirror this process by gradually deepening the conversation over time, leading to:

- **Deeper exploration**: Respondents are encouraged to dig further into the topic, moving beyond surface-level answers.
- **Greater clarity**: As the conversation evolves, you can address points of confusion or refine earlier responses.
- **Nuanced perspectives**: Through iterative questioning, respondents are more likely to consider multiple viewpoints and develop a more well-rounded perspective.
- **Continuous engagement**: Iterative dialogue keeps the conversation active and engaging, allowing for a richer exchange of ideas.

How to Build Iterative Dialogue

Designing iterative dialogue requires careful planning to ensure that each prompt builds naturally on the last while encouraging deeper exploration of the topic. Here's how to construct a series of prompts that create an effective iterative dialogue:

---

1. Start Broad, Then Narrow the Focus

The first step in iterative dialogue is to begin with a **broad** prompt that opens up the conversation and invites general exploration of the topic. Once the respondent provides their initial answer, you can narrow the focus with follow-up questions that ask for **clarification**, **examples**, or **further exploration**.

Example:

- **Initial Prompt**: *"How do you think AI will impact the future of work?"*

➡ This broad prompt invites respondents to share their general thoughts on AI and work.

- **Follow-Up Prompt**: *"You mentioned that AI could lead to job displacement. What types of jobs do you think are most at risk, and what skills will be important to mitigate these risks?"*

➡ This follow-up narrows the focus by asking the respondent to identify specific jobs and skills, encouraging deeper thinking.

---

2. Incorporate Reflection on Previous Responses

As the conversation progresses, it's important to encourage respondents to **reflect on their earlier answers**. This not only deepens the dialogue but also invites the respondent to **reconsider** or **refine** their original thoughts, leading to more thoughtful, evolved responses.

Example:

- **Reflection Prompt**: *"Earlier, you mentioned that AI could improve workplace efficiency. However, do you see any potential downsides to this, such as employee engagement or decision-making transparency?"*

➡ This prompt refers back to the respondent's initial response (workplace efficiency) while encouraging them to explore **potential downsides**, leading to a more balanced answer.

---

3. Use Probing Questions to Encourage Depth

Probing questions are designed to push the respondent to **go beyond their initial answer** by asking them to explain, justify, or analyze their response in greater detail. These types of questions encourage **critical thinking** and **introspection**, leading to more insightful answers.

Example:

• **Probing Prompt**: *"You mentioned that implementing AI could streamline decision-making processes. Could you explain how this might work in practice? What challenges might arise in terms of fairness or bias in decision-making?"*

➡ This prompt asks the respondent to **explain the practical application** of their initial answer and then introduces a new layer (fairness and bias), deepening the conversation.

---

4. Explore Multiple Perspectives

To foster a more nuanced conversation, use iterative prompts to explore the topic from **multiple angles** or **perspectives**. This encourages respondents to think more broadly about the issue and consider **different viewpoints** or **trade-offs**.

Example:

• **Perspective Prompt**: *"You've discussed the potential benefits of AI in the workplace. How do you think AI might impact employees at different levels of the company, from entry-level workers to executives?"*

➡ This prompt invites the respondent to explore how AI affects **different stakeholders**, leading to a more comprehensive response.

---

5. Introduce New Dimensions to the Conversation

Once you've explored the topic in depth, you can introduce **new dimensions** to the conversation that challenge the respondent to think in new ways or consider **unexplored aspects** of the issue.

Example:

- **New Dimension Prompt**: *"Beyond its impact on the workplace, how do you think AI could shape the broader economy or societal structures in the next decade?"*

➡ This prompt broadens the conversation by moving from the **workplace context** to the **broader economy**, encouraging the respondent to think about the **wider implications** of AI.

Creating an Iterative Dialogue Flow

Here's a step-by-step example of how an iterative dialogue might unfold, building deeper insights at each stage.

Topic: The Role of AI in Healthcare

---

1. **Broad Opening Prompt**:
   "How do you think AI is changing the healthcare industry?"
   ➡ This broad question invites the respondent to share their general thoughts on AI in healthcare, encouraging a wide range of responses.

---

2. **Follow-Up to Narrow Focus**:
   "You mentioned that AI could improve diagnostic accuracy. Can you provide an example of how AI might be used in diagnostic tools, and what benefits this could bring to patient care?"
   ➡ This follow-up narrows the focus to a specific application of AI (diagnostics) and asks the respondent to provide a more detailed example.

---

3. **Reflection and Exploration of Risks**:
   "While AI might improve diagnostics, are there any potential risks or limitations that concern you, such as patient data privacy or over-reliance on AI systems?"
   ➡ This prompt encourages the respondent to reflect on **risks or limitations**, balancing their initial response with potential downsides.

4. **Probing for Depth**:
   "You mentioned concerns about patient data privacy. How might healthcare providers mitigate these risks, and what role could regulation play in ensuring data security?"
   ➡ This probing question digs deeper into the **specific issue** of data privacy, asking the respondent to think about **solutions** and **regulatory measures**.

5. **Introducing New Perspectives**:
   "Beyond diagnostics, how might AI change the role of healthcare professionals? Could AI take over certain tasks, or would it require a rethinking of how doctors and AI systems collaborate?"
   ➡ This prompt introduces a new angle—AI's impact on **healthcare professionals**—inviting the respondent to think about how AI could affect the **workforce** and collaboration.

6. **Expanding the Scope**:
   "Looking further ahead, how do you see AI shaping global healthcare systems over the next decade? What challenges or opportunities might arise as AI becomes more integrated into healthcare delivery?"
   ➡ This final prompt broadens the scope to a **global**

perspective, encouraging the respondent to think about the long-term implications of AI in healthcare.

The Benefits of Iterative Dialogue

1. **Deepening Understanding**: By building on previous answers, iterative dialogue encourages respondents to explore topics in more depth, leading to a more **comprehensive** understanding of the issue.
2. **Evolving Ideas**: Respondents can reflect on and **refine** their initial ideas as the conversation progresses, leading to more thoughtful and evolved answers.
3. **Exploring Complexities**: Through probing and reflection, iterative dialogue helps uncover the **complexities** of a topic, leading to more nuanced perspectives.
4. **Building Engagement**: Continuous engagement through follow-up questions keeps the conversation dynamic and interactive, preventing the dialogue from becoming stale.

Conclusion: The Power of Iterative Dialogue

Iterative dialogue is a powerful tool for fostering **meaningful, in-depth conversations** that evolve over time. By building prompts that respond to earlier answers, probe for more detail, and introduce new perspectives, you create a dynamic exchange that leads to deeper insights and more thoughtful responses. This method helps unlock the full potential of dialogue, allowing both the respondent and the prompt designer to explore ideas in a more **collaborative, reflective** way.

In the next chapter, we'll discuss **strategic flexibility**—how to remain adaptable and adjust your prompts in real-time to ensure you achieve the best possible responses during a dynamic conversation. This final chapter will explore the importance of flexibility in prompt design and how to use it to maintain engagement, steer the dialogue effectively, and adapt to unexpected turns.

CHAPTER 16: STRATEGIC FLEXIBILITY – ADAPTING PROMPTS IN REAL-TIME

No matter how well you design a prompt, the flow of conversation can be **unpredictable**. Strategic flexibility means being prepared to **adjust** your prompts based on the respondent's answers and the direction the conversation takes. This real-time adaptability helps ensure that the dialogue remains **engaging**, **focused**, and **productive**, even when things go off track or when new opportunities for exploration arise.

In this chapter, we'll explore how to stay flexible in your prompt strategy, when and how to adjust prompts in the middle of a conversation, and how to maintain momentum without losing focus.

Why Strategic Flexibility Matters

Conversations, especially deep or complex ones, are rarely **linear**. Respondents might interpret a prompt in unexpected ways, offer new insights you didn't anticipate, or take the conversation in a direction that requires further exploration. Strategic flexibility ensures that you're able to:

- **Maintain engagement**: If the conversation drifts or stalls, flexibility allows you to bring it back on track.

- **Explore new avenues**: When respondents introduce fresh ideas or unexpected insights, you can adjust your prompts to dive deeper into these new areas.
- **Clarify misunderstandings**: If the respondent misinterprets a prompt, flexibility allows you to quickly reframe the question to ensure clarity and focus.

By staying flexible, you can guide the conversation without being rigid, making it more **dynamic** and **responsive** to the flow of the dialogue.

When to Adjust Your Prompts

There are several situations where adjusting your prompts in real-time can significantly enhance the quality of the conversation:

1. **When the response is too vague or broad**:
   Sometimes, respondents may give an answer that's too general or not focused enough. In this case, adjusting the prompt to **narrow the scope** or ask for clarification can help bring the conversation back to a more productive line of thinking.
   Example:

   ○ **Initial Prompt**: *"How can technology improve team collaboration?"*
   ○ **Vague Response**: *"It makes it easier to share ideas."*
   ○ **Adjusted Prompt**: *"Can you give a specific example of how a tool like Slack or Zoom has improved collaboration on your team?"*

---

2. **When the response opens up new insights**:
   A great conversation can uncover unexpected insights or reveal perspectives you hadn't considered. In these cases, being flexible allows you to **seize the opportunity** and dig deeper into these new ideas.
   Example:

   ○ **Initial Prompt**: *"What are the advantages of remote work?"*

- New Insight in Response: *"It allows for a more global workforce."*
- Adjusted Prompt: *"That's interesting—how do you think having a global workforce affects company culture or communication styles?"*

---

3. **When the conversation stalls**:
   If the conversation hits a roadblock or the respondent seems unsure how to answer, adjusting your prompt to **rephrase the question**, provide examples, or shift focus can help keep the dialogue moving.
   Example:

- Initial Prompt: *"What role do you think AI will play in the future of education?"*
- Stalled Response: *"I'm not sure, there are so many possibilities."*
- Adjusted Prompt: *"Let's narrow it down. How do you think AI could help teachers manage large classrooms or personalize learning for students?"*

---

4. **When the response goes off track**:
   Respondents may sometimes interpret a question differently than you intended and take the conversation in an unrelated direction. In this case, gently **redirecting** the prompt can bring the focus back to the key topic.
   Example:

- Initial Prompt: *"What are some challenges companies face when adopting green technologies?"*
- Off-Track Response: *"There's also the issue of AI in the workplace…"*
- Adjusted Prompt: *"That's an important point, but I'd like to focus on green technologies for now. What specific barriers do you think companies encounter when trying to go green?"*

Techniques for Adjusting Prompts in Real-Time

Here are some practical techniques for making effective adjustments to your prompts during a conversation, keeping the dialogue flexible yet focused.

1. Rephrase or Reframe the Question

If the respondent seems unsure how to answer or misunderstands the prompt, a simple **rephrasing** or **reframing** of the question can clarify your intent and help guide the conversation in the right direction.

Example:

- **Initial Prompt**: *"What are the main challenges of digital transformation?"*
- **Adjusted Prompt**: *"When a company adopts digital tools, what challenges do you think they face in terms of training employees or changing workflows?"*

➡ Reframing the prompt focuses on **specific aspects** (training, workflows), making it easier for the respondent to engage.

2. Ask for Examples or Specifics

If the response is too broad or general, asking for specific examples or details helps add **depth** to the conversation and brings more clarity to the respondent's ideas.

Example:

- **General Response**: *"Remote work makes it easier for teams to communicate."*
- **Adjusted Prompt**: *"Can you give an example of a tool or method that has improved communication in your team since going remote?"*

➡ This encourages the respondent to provide a **real-world example**, leading to a more focused and concrete answer.

---

3. Shift Focus to a Different Aspect

If the conversation seems to be going in circles or has exhausted a particular line of thinking, shifting the focus to a **different aspect** of the topic can open up new areas for exploration.

Example:

- **Initial Focus**: *"How can AI improve customer service?"*
- **Adjusted Focus**: *"We've talked about improving response times—how might AI help personalize customer interactions and make them feel more connected to the brand?"*

➡ This shifts the conversation to a **new dimension** (personalization), keeping the dialogue fresh and engaging.

---

4. Introduce Contrasts or Comparisons

When a conversation feels stagnant or the responses lack depth, introducing a **comparison** or **contrast** can help spark deeper thinking. Asking respondents to weigh the pros and cons or compare different options keeps the conversation dynamic.

Example:

- **Original Prompt**: *"How can technology help manage remote teams?"*
- **Adjusted Prompt**: *"How does managing a remote team differ from managing an in-office team, and what specific challenges do you think technology can help overcome in each case?"*

➡ By introducing a **comparison**, the respondent is encouraged to think more critically and offer a more detailed response.

Balancing Flexibility with Focus

While being flexible in your prompts is essential, it's also important not to let the conversation **wander too far** from your original objectives. Strategic flexibility means balancing openness with the need to **stay on track**. Here's how to strike that balance:

---

1. Set Clear Goals for the Conversation

Before starting the conversation, have a clear understanding of the **core objectives**. This ensures that even if you adjust the prompts, the conversation remains aligned with your goals.

Example:

- If the goal is to explore how AI impacts **employee engagement**, make sure that even when the conversation shifts to broader discussions about AI, you periodically steer it back to focus on **engagement**.

---

2. Use Gentle Redirects

When the conversation drifts too far off topic, use **gentle redirects** to bring it back in line. Acknowledge the respondent's point, but subtly shift the focus back to the original theme.

Example:

- **Off-Track Response**: *"That reminds me of how AI is affecting healthcare…"*
- **Gentle Redirect**: *"That's an interesting connection. For now, let's focus on the workplace side of AI. What challenges do you think arise when it's applied to employee training?"*

---

3. Keep Key Themes in Mind

As the conversation evolves, keep track of the **key themes** or ideas that are central to the discussion. When making adjustments, refer back to these themes to ensure the conversation remains cohesive.

Example:

- If a key theme is **sustainability**, make sure that even when exploring different angles—such as economic or technological aspects—you regularly connect the dialogue back to sustainability.

Conclusion: Mastering Strategic Flexibility

Strategic flexibility is about being **responsive** and **adaptable** in the moment while still maintaining control over the flow of the conversation. By adjusting your prompts in real-time, you can keep the dialogue engaging, explore unexpected insights, and steer respondents back to focus when necessary. Flexibility in prompt design allows for a more **organic** and **productive** conversation, leading to richer and more insightful responses.

This final chapter underscores the importance of adaptability in effective prompt design, reminding us that the art of conversation is not about rigid control, but about knowing when to guide, when to explore, and when to adjust.